T0347069

A Fake Saint and the True Church

A Fake Saint and the True Church

The Story of a Forgery in Seventeenth-Century Naples

STEFANIA TUTINO

OXFORD

UNIVERSITY PRESS

OXFORD
UNIVERSITY PRESS

Oxford University Press is a department of the University of Oxford. It furthers the University's objective of excellence in research, scholarship, and education by publishing worldwide. Oxford is a registered trade mark of Oxford University Press in the UK and certain other countries.

Published in the United States of America by Oxford University Press
198 Madison Avenue, New York, NY 10016, United States of America.

Library of Congress Control Number: 2021941756
ISBN 978-0-19-757880-3

DOI: 10.1093/oso/9780197578803.001.0001

1 3 5 7 9 8 6 4 2

Printed by Sheridan Books, Inc., United States of America

Contents

Acknowledgments

As I write, we are in the middle of the coronavirus pandemic, which is destroying the life of thousands of people and the livelihood of millions of families throughout the world. In addition, all of us in the United States (I truly hope) are outraged and horrified by the racial, social, and economic injustices and inequities of our country, which the murder of George Floyd has put, yet again, into stark relief. Now more than ever, I realize how lucky and privileged I am, and how much I have to be grateful for. So it is a particular pleasure for me to thank all the people who have made it possible for me to write this book, starting with the staff of the libraries and archives in which I worked. I am especially grateful to Fabrizio de Sibi and Daniel Ponziani at the ACDF, Martín Morales and Lorenzo Mancini at the APUG, Mauro Brunello and Salvatore Vassallo at the ARSI, and the staff of the AAV and BAV. I am also grateful to the John Simon Guggenheim Memorial Foundation for providing much-needed time to bring this book to completion.

Several colleagues and friends have read the manuscript, offered comments and criticisms, suggested corrections, and provided support and encouragement. Among them I would especially like to mention Tommaso Astarita, Simon Ditchfield, Constantin Fasolt, Mordechai Feingold, Anthony Grafton, Lisa Halttunen, Anthony Milton, Alexandra Walsham, as well as the anonymous readers from the press. I would also like to acknowledge the support of my colleagues at UCLA, and especially Peg Jacob, Lynn Hunt, and Teo Ruiz, as well as the chairs of my department, Stephen Aron and Carla Pestana. My editor at OUP, Cynthia Read, has always been extraordinarily generous with her time and attention, even in difficult times. Her dedication to authors and their books is exemplary and I am fortunate to work with her.

I am immensely grateful to my family and my friends; I genuinely have no words to thank them for standing by my side when I needed it the most. My son Tiziano Treu-Tutino has been a trouper. He met the challenges that these tough circumstances brought to his all-important toddler routine with good humor, love, and the occasional tantrum, which reminded his parents that it is ok sometimes to feel sad, angry, and upset. My husband Tommaso Treu has been at the center of my life for more than twenty years. In these last months, we faced some good days and some bad days. I am infinitely grateful for being able to share both the joys and the burdens.

Finally, I said that I have written this book with my students in mind, and I mean it in the most literal and concrete sense of this expression. I have assigned some of the sources I use in this book in my fall 2019 proseminar, and I have shared my drafts with the students so that they could criticize and discuss my arguments, just as I did with their research papers. Their comments were eye-opening and their questions were refreshing. Their infinite curiosity to know more about topics I initially hadn't considered worthy of attention has been a source of pride and joy for me, and a reminder that I am so very lucky to have the privilege of teaching for a living. It is with immense gratitude that I acknowledge these students from my fall 2019 proseminar by name: Annica Denktas, Allie LaPierre Davies, AJ Maloney, David Mendoza, Cole North, Erik Renner, Madeline Samson, Noga Tour, Cristian Walk.

Introduction

Among the undergraduate courses that I regularly teach, there is one devoted to the Roman Inquisition, which I like to offer as a seminar to first-year students. On the first day of class, I always ask my students what they already know about the topic. The responses I have gotten over the years usually amount to a combination of the same three elements. First, according to my students, the Roman Inquisitors, and early modern Catholic society in general, were unfathomably determined to defend the truth of Catholic dogmas at all costs. Second, they believe that the first point—the apparent fact that early modern Catholic leaders defended their beliefs without considering any reasonable evidence to the contrary or indeed the laws of nature—proves that the epistemological standards of the early modern Catholic Church were crude and primitive. Finally, they tend to believe that early modern Inquisitors were not only dogmatic and cognitively deficient but also morally evil, hell-bent on destroying the lives of their victims, whose only fault, as the students see it, was to defend truth and rationality in the face of mindless superstition. Here, of course, the image of Galileo Galilei as a martyr for modern science inevitably pops up.

Over the course of the class, my students gather some background on the religious history of early modern Europe, read some of the most recent literature on the institutional, social, cultural, and theological place of the Roman Inquisition within the early modern Catholic world, examine an array of primary sources from different Inquisitorial trials (including Galileo's), and produce a short essay analyzing a primary source. Ideally, all of this work

A Fake Saint and the True Church. Stefania Tutino, Oxford University Press. © Oxford University Press 2021. DOI: 10.1093/oso/9780197578803.003.0001

gives them not only a better sense of the historical significance of the Roman Inquisition, but also the opportunity to appreciate the nuts and bolts of the historical method.

On the last day of class, I ask whether they have learned something they did not know before. Invariably, all of them report that they have. To be sure, in the space of ten weeks, not all of them acquire a solid, let alone strong, command of the context within which the dogmatism of early modern Catholic society needs to be considered. Few demonstrate a full appreciation of the epistemological sophistication involved in the process of early modern Catholic censorship. And, despite the new historical skills they learn in class and my best efforts to highlight the difference between historical evaluation and moral judgment, I fear that many of them retain the notion that early modern Inquisitors were evil people. Nevertheless, what all of my students learn (to varying degrees) is that, contrary to their initial beliefs, the Roman Inquisitors were not necessarily crazy and pitifully irrational. They begin to see that the reality was more complicated than they thought it was, and realize that the neat boxes into which they used to sort their knowledge of early modern Catholicism have become too small to contain the newly acquired information.

This newfound awareness does not erase the distance my students feel between the present and the past. In fact, in some sense it intensifies it. At the end of the course, they still find the early modern Catholic world utterly foreign and different from their own, and they still believe that the lives of the Inquisitors and their victims couldn't be more alien to those of a twenty-first-century American college student. What "sticks," however, is the realization that the reason for this difference cannot be ascribed to some congenital deficiency that prevented early modern people from becoming wholly rational (and consequently fully modern) —a deficiency that was then almost magically erased by the advent of a semi-mythical "modern secular reason." They begin to grasp that the reasons for the distance between the present and the past lie in a mix of political, social, religious, cultural, and intellectual factors, which can and should be understood and explained in properly historical terms.

Many of my students have no desire to pursue the matter any further, and go on to take courses in other subjects within or outside the history department. Yet, at the end of the course, I am always very satisfied with the results. To paraphrase the Earl of Kent in Shakespeare's *King Lear* (and Wittgenstein), I believe that one of the most important goals for a historian is to teach differences. Seeing students begin to identify and appreciate historical differences is immensely rewarding, both personally and professionally.

My students' initial prejudices concerning the Roman Inquisition stem in part from the increasingly peripheral place that the history of pre-modern Europe occupies in American high school curricula. Their prejudices are also the (more or less conscious) manifestation of a very common attitude toward the past—that is, to see it as a function of the present, with the present being the inevitable *telos* of history. Just as in the case of my students approaching the Roman Inquisition, this attitude usually presents itself in a triumphalist, vaguely Hegelian, mode. The present is viewed as the culmination of a long and tortuous journey through violence, inequality, and ignorance; based on this reference point, the past is nothing but a collection of obstacles that modern Western society had to overcome before the present could be fully realized.

At times, another manifestation appears, in which the triumphalist mode is abandoned in favor of a nostalgic one: the present is full of horrors and atrocities, and the promise of a free, peaceful, and bountiful future for all humanity has been all but betrayed. Thus, we turn to the past to discover that pre-modern people were not always worse than we are. In fact, they might have been better: more connected to their communities, more respectful of their environment, and less prone to murder each other on a massive scale. From the perspective of present society, I think that seeing the past as a function of the present is not necessarily a mistake; it might be an interesting way to identify and express our own current values. I personally believe that condemning violence and ignorance, working to create a more equitable, just, and peaceful society, and fighting to save the planet are all commendable goals. If some of us need to enlist the past to strengthen our commitment to the future, so be it (although we should all be conscious of the fact that by this same logic, the past has been invoked to justify not only peace and justice, but also white supremacy, racism, and intolerance).

Yet, if the goal is to understand the past rather than co-opt it as an unwitting ally in a crusade to change the world, this obsession with measuring how much better or worse the past was with respect to the present is wrong-headed. It prevents us from understanding and respecting the extent to which the past is first and foremost *different*. In addition to helping us get a better grasp on history, I believe that understanding how the past is different from the present is an excellent way to understand our own society. But I am a historian after all, and while I gladly concede that not everybody thinks as I do about the value of history, I do feel the duty to teach my students what history is. This means teaching them differences.

I wrote this book with my students in mind. I imagine that other people might harbor the same misconceptions about early modern Catholic culture, and that they might be just as happy to learn something they did not know before. More specifically, I wrote this book to show that early modern Catholic culture was not the apex of superstition and obscurantism, destined to be overcome by modern secular rationality. The reality is more complicated. Many early modern Catholic leaders, theologians, and intellectuals knew how to gather and evaluate evidence, how to appreciate the strength of opinions and arguments, and how to distinguish the authentic from the fake. In sum, many could use their reason as effectively and appropriately as people can today.

Yet, the context in which early modern Catholic theologians exercised their reasoning capacity was different from our own. To begin with, early modern people lived in a cultural, intellectual, and social environment in which human truths coexisted with supernatural truths; therefore the presence of the divine was not only the center of their daily lives but also the foundation of their epistemological universe. But the fact that religion occupied a central place in early modern Europe does not mean that all early modern Europeans were congenitally more liable than we are to be exploited by someone who took advantage of their "mindless credulity." Naturally, some people then were better equipped than others to distinguish between reasonable and unreasonable claims, just as they are today. While the criteria that early modern people used to evaluate what was reasonable and what wasn't were not much different from our own, early modern people did have a different set of priorities and were confronted by a different set of challenges when it came to the relationship between true, reasonable, and authentic.

My book seeks to explain those differences through a seventeenth-century case of forged sanctity that provoked an intricate and dramatic twenty-year debate in the Roman Curia over the authenticity of certain documents. The protagonist of this story is Carlo Calà, Duke of Diano, a Neapolitan jurist and high-ranking officer of the viceregal administration. In the middle of the seventeenth century, Carlo began to promote the cult of a supposed holy ancestor by the name of Giovanni Calà. Said to have lived in Calabria between the twelfth and the thirteenth centuries, Giovanni Calà served the Holy Roman Emperor Henry VI as one of his most trusted army captains, aiding the emperor in conquering southern Italy. Despite his military accomplishments, however, Giovanni abruptly gave up his secular life and became a hermit after a miraculous encounter with an angel. Rewarded by God with extraordinary charisma, Giovanni enjoyed the gift of prophecy and was the author of several miracles, before dying a holy death sometime in the first half of the thirteenth century.

Giovanni's feats, and his very existence, were completely unknown until the 1650s, when a substantial collection of documents began to appear. These told the amazing story of Giovanni's military prowess, sudden conversion, saintly prophetic spirit, and supernatural ability to perform miracles. The problem was that the documents were forged. We still do not know whether the Duke of Diano, Giovanni's seventeenth-century descendant, actively participated in the forgery or was simply the credulous victim of it. We do know that he defended the authenticity of the documents and used them extensively in two treatises he wrote to bolster the case for canonizing his ancestor. The duke was aided by the viceroy, the highest political authority in the kingdom of Naples, who used the duke's fictitious ancestor to advance his own interests vis-à-vis the Roman Curia and the local Neapolitan clergy.

Soon after the duke began his promotional campaign, the case of Giovanni made its way to the Congregation of the Index of Prohibited Books, which investigated the authenticity of the documents and the duke's role in disseminating them. Even though many scholars and theologians in the Roman Curia suspected that the story of Giovanni was a forgery, they also realized that the Roman Church did not quite know how to deal with the relationship between historical authenticity and theological orthodoxy. Catholic leaders debated the case of the fake prophet Giovanni for two decades, never reaching a final decision on how to reconcile the truth of history with the supernatural truth of theology and the devotional needs of the Church.

I believe that Giovanni's case is worth exploring today because it exposes fundamental and uncomfortable questions. How much can the truth of doctrine depend on the truth of historical facts before theology loses its ontological autonomy and becomes simply a branch of ecclesiastical history or philological criticism? To what extent can the truth of doctrine ignore the truth of the facts without becoming engulfed in falsity and deceit? Behind the anxiety that the Roman hierarchy manifested toward the Duke of Diano and his fictitious holy ancestor lie larger and more knotty questions concerning the nature of Catholic theology in its relationship to a central feature of modernity. How can the absolute truth of theology engage with the far less absolute certainty of human affairs? How can the supernatural survive as both a normative system and a hermeneutical principle in a world that is increasingly dominated by the human?

Carlo Calà's attempts to construct an impressive (and fictitious) genealogy are by no means unique in early modern Europe. Instances of forged saints and relics are virtually omnipresent in post-Tridentine Catholicism. Yet few, if any, other cases of individual forgery provoked such long and dramatic debate within the Roman Curia. Building on Arnaldo Momigliano's seminal reflections on the place of erudition within the Western intellectual tradition, and on Anthony Grafton's crucial contributions to the study of the cultural, historical, and intellectual significance of forgeries, I use this fascinating case study to explore several important features of early modern (and modern) European culture.

First, current scholarship on early modern Catholicism (including my own) has demonstrated that the Roman Curia was not a monolithic institution. It was a multiform, internally divided, and intellectually dynamic venue for debate and conflict. This book shows how different institutional and intellectual voices within the Roman Curia tried to address—in often conflicting ways— fundamental questions such as the political role of the papacy in the context of the emerging nation states, the epistemological future of Catholic theology in the context of the developing scientific and critical attitude, and the place of Catholic devotion to miracles and saints in the context of an emerging secular understanding of evidence and credibility.

Second, the case of Giovanni attests to the complexity of the relationship between political and religious authority in the delicate equilibrium of power between the Roman center and local Catholic communities. The Duke of Diano enjoyed significant authority within the Neapolitan administration, whose relationship with the Roman Curia was politically and religiously complicated. From this perspective, the story of the duke and his fake holy ancestor was a quintessentially Neapolitan (that is, "provincial") story of social mobility and political leverage, and the Roman reaction to it was an attempt by the papacy to prevent Neapolitan political leaders from using saints and miracles to advance their political ambitions. This case can therefore serve as a magnifying lens to better understand the relationship between political legitimacy and religious authority, the tension between the goals of the Roman center and the needs of the local Catholic communities, and the intricacies of the political landscape of the early modern Italian peninsula.

Third, this book sheds new light on the relationship between historical criticism and theological commitment. The work of Simon Ditchfield, Anthony Grafton, and Jean-Louis Quantin, among others, has demonstrated that ecclesiastical erudition was far from immune to post-Humanist philological and historical criticism. This newly critical attitude toward saints and miracles often came into tension with the Catholic Church's theological commitment to the absolute truth of doctrine. Once the methods and techniques to sort out the truth of history became more sophisticated, the defense of the truth of theology became more epistemologically, politically, and intellectually complex. This book contributes to this line of inquiry by showing that the rise of modern criticism was developed in conversation with, not in opposition to, faith in the supernatural. Given that our own society still struggles to come to terms with the relationship between the natural and the supernatural, this story is all the more relevant.

Finally, the controversy over the authenticity of the sources attesting to Giovanni's life and deeds caused a profound debate concerning the nature of legal and historical documents as evidence of the truth of the past. The story of Giovanni forced many seventeenth-century erudites, theologians, and jurists to reflect on the extent to which legal documents preserved in the archive could function as *historical* evidence, and on the role that record-keeping, evidence, and proof play in verifying the authenticity of the past. This book contributes to a vibrant scholarly debate seeking to rethink the notions of record and evidence in the context of the relationship between history, memory, and truth. I believe that investigating the early modern understanding of evidence and proof is not only historically significant but also exceedingly timely, as we are still deeply invested in examining the difference between evidence, facts, truths, and opinions.

From a methodological viewpoint, this book fits the historiographical category of microhistory—its object of analysis is a small, "micro" episode in the history of early modern Catholicism, as opposed to large-scale or "macro" units, trends, or developments. As readers will soon realize, it decidedly foregrounds the narrative mode, keeping the analysis in the background. Since the pioneering work of Carlo Ginzburg, Giovanni Levi, and Natalie Zemon Davis, numerous historians have demonstrated the methodological advantages of microhistorical analysis, even in the current age of world history and global approaches. Since the advent of the so-called linguistic turn, which stirred historians to pay special attention to the potentialities and limitations of language in relation to knowledge and truth, many works have shown the heuristic benefits of a narrative approach to historical investigations, both micro and macro. A substantial number of other historians have already defended microhistorical and narrative historiography better than I could do myself, but I want to state more explicitly why I decided to write this book in the way I did.

To begin with, I realize that the ideological and cultural context in which the first proponents of microhistory worked is very different from the context in which I work. Although they used different sources, considered different subjects, and had different scholarly agendas, the first wave of microhistorians, especially in Italy, shared an ideological commitment: to reject the notion of history as a constant march toward progress and instead highlight the *cost* of liberalism and capitalism. This ideological posture led the first microhistorians to focus on the specific, the idiosyncratic, or the "exceptionally normal," as Edoardo Grendi put it. The aim was less to recover how "real people" lived than to magnify all the problems, incongruences, and disruptions that macrohistorical paradigms and methods tended to ignore.

Today, things are different. My generation (when the first Italian edition of *The Cheese and the Worms* came out, in 1976, I wasn't yet born) is no longer *dis*-illusioned with the linear trajectory culminating in the triumph of the liberal, modern, and consumeristic society. We never got the opportunity to cultivate any illusion in the first place. Moreover, since the 1990s and especially the 2000s, the historical profession has seen a profound "democratization," as Lynn Hunt wrote, of both its practitioners and its subject matter. Consequently, while in the 1970s and early 1980s microhistorians could still be considered methodological rebels who opposed the way of doing history that was proper to "organic" intellectuals, as Gramsci would have put it, today a critic could argue that one of the reasons microhistory is ill-suited to understanding global questions is its implicit Eurocentrism.

Although I do not share my microhistorian predecessors' ideology, I do share their commitment to an intensive, and even intimate, relationship with primary sources. Carlo Ginzburg used to tell us in class that sources needed to be "*spremute,*" or "squeezed" (I find it interesting that, as Francesca Trivellato reports, Giovanni Levi used this same verb with his own students). Ginzburg accompanied the words with the appropriate gesture, one hand pressing hard on the other. Today, when I speak to my own students, I try to convey Ginzburg's sense of urgency about primary sources by expanding the verb into a more intricate (and certainly less elegant) metaphor. Imagine, I tell my students, that you have just completed a marathon, and when you get to the finish line, you find not a bottle of water or Gatorade, but only a single orange waiting for you. Similarly, when you get to the archive, *squeeze* your sources as hard as you would squeeze that orange if you knew that its juice was the only thing you could drink after your run.

This book was born out of my attempt to squeeze the sources. I was reading the Holy Office's *Decreta* (the minutes of the weekly meetings of the Inquisitors), looking for something else, when suddenly a few references to the story of Carlo and Giovanni Calà popped up. I ignored the first two references (the terse and repetitive format in which decisions, events, people, and cases were recorded in the *Decreta* makes it easy to ignore what you aren't looking for). But the third time Carlo Calà's name was mentioned within the span of a couple of weeks, like Marc Bloch's ogre I caught the scent of human flesh and became curious to know more. I found it odd that the Inquisitors would spend so much time discussing an unknown (to me, at least) character. So, like a truffle hunter (and I take no offense at this image), I began to search. I discovered that even though the story of the fake prophet and his ambitious seventeenth-century descendant is a "micro" event in the world of post-Reformation Catholicism, it is particularly well-suited to making connections with the larger context and challenging our understanding of post-Reformation Catholic culture.

Despite my initial ignorance, I realized that the case of Carlo and Giovanni Calà is uncommonly well-documented. To be sure, we do not have a complete, finite, and neatly arranged set of documents centered on Carlo Calà, and most of the evidence concerning this story is scattered throughout different types of sources. Despite the inevitable holes, however, it is possible to reconstruct quite a detailed picture of what happened in this case. This provides an exceptional opportunity to test the limits of what we think we know about the process of Catholic censorship.

Furthermore, the affair of the fake prophet Giovanni had remarkably wide implications. Because of the social, religious, political, and cultural backgrounds in which the story unfolded, the case of Giovanni Calà allows us to deepen our knowledge of post-Tridentine Catholic censorship and the relationship between truth and authenticity in the early modern Roman Curia. It also enables us to investigate the precarious equilibrium of power in the Neapolitan government, the tension between the institutional factions within the papacy, and the intellectual and social dynamics in the early modern cultural, political, and religious elites.

I believe that at its core, microhistory is not about focusing on the small, but rather about putting a particular case in constant dialogue with the larger context, thus exposing and exploring connections at different scales. Thus I thought that the story of Carlo Calà and his fake ancestor was an excellent subject for a microhistorical analysis that simultaneously presupposes and enriches the larger context. Moreover, since I know that the most inspired microhistorians use the micro to tell something big about history, I have sought to follow their example by using this story and its multifarious connections to tell something interesting about the big questions of evidence, truth, and belief.

Concerning the narrative approach of this book, I have embraced it for several reasons. First, one of the most interesting features of the story of Carlo Calà and his fake ancestor is the extent to which it is linked to several other, seemingly very different, contexts and questions. At the beginning, I felt a bit disoriented by the many directions in which this story unfolded: from the cloistered walls of the Roman Curia to the messy scene of early modern Neapolitan politics; from the science of volcanic eruptions to the history of medieval hermits; from debates over the significance of legal evidence to debates over the authenticity of ancient manuscripts. Nevertheless, once I decided to just go with the flow, as it were, I found that embracing these centrifugal forces allowed me to learn much more than I had anticipated. I enjoyed the process tremendously and believed that a narrative approach would enable other people to feel the same enjoyment that I felt. Even by focusing on one relatively obscure episode in the history of seventeenth-century Catholicism, it is possible to gain a wide and deep picture of several theological, political, cultural, and intellectual features of the early modern Catholic world. I hope that reading about these different people and issues piques the readers' curiosity and stirs them to further research.

Another reason that I decided to foreground narrative has to do with the dialectic between knowledge and ignorance that underlies all historical investigations. In other words, this is the relationship between "proofs and possibilities," as Carlo Ginzburg wrote concerning Natalie Zemon Davis's narrative strategy in *The Return of Martin Guerre*. Every time I go into an archive, I feel an exhilarating mixture of excitement and anxiety, because I am sure that I will find *something*. On the one hand, I have full confidence, faith even, that I will find some trace of the past among the documents. I know that far too many people and events have been completely obliterated by the passage of time, but I also know that an archive, by definition, is a repository of what survives; therefore it must contain at least some clues, signs, and vestiges of the reality of the past.

On the other hand, I also know that no matter what I find, I will not find everything. Aside from the inevitable shortcomings of my human flesh-smelling and truffle-hunting instincts, I know that documents get lost, folders survive in pieces and bits, records are never transparent representations of reality, and the record-keepers themselves sometimes fail to record something, either because they thought it wasn't important or because they wanted to avoid leaving a written trace of it. Besides, no matter how comprehensive the evidence, no surviving record will ever tell you how people truly felt when they heard the pope's sentence of condemnation or saw Mount Vesuvius erupt. Taking stock of the inevitable gaps in my knowledge makes me anxious, not because I wish these gaps didn't exist, but because I want to do them justice. I don't want to erase them by pretending that what I do know is perfectly smooth and continuous, or by artificially filling them without letting the reader know the difference between historical truth and historical imagination. Thus I am anxious to find a way to be honest with my readers about what I know and what I don't, and to present what I have in a way that respects both the coherence of my interpretation and the porosity of my knowledge. Once again, the methodological insight of the pioneers of microhistory has come to my rescue. Following in their footsteps, in this book I have decided to use narrative to simultaneously give justice to the truth of the documents and to exercise my historical imagination without blurring the line between them.

To explain why I believe that I can, and in some cases should, exercise my historical imagination provided that I keep it distinct from the truth that I find in the documents, I will not invoke the debate concerning relativism, narrative, and truth-telling in historiography. Those who are familiar with my past scholarship already know how I feel about it: appreciating the creative role of narrative and aiming to provide a truthful account of the past are not a zero-sum game; recognizing that the historian's account of the past is the only means to bring to life what is, in effect, dead does not mean giving up on the goal of telling the truth. But rather than providing a fuller historiographical discussion about these issues, I think a short story about my grandfather will suffice to clarify my position.

My grandfather, Antonio Gilona, was born poor in a village in Sicily. When he was a young man, right after marrying my grandmother, he was sent to fight in WWII, on the Russian front. He came back alive, although his face and body were horribly disfigured. When he returned, he found a job in a cement factory, and after he retired, he bought a small piece of land, where he spent all his time alone, tending to his lemon trees, tomatoes, zucchini, and the occasional chicken that he kept because of the eggs. He died of cancer (a common occurrence among cement-factory workers) when I was a teenager, and too young and self-absorbed for his death to affect me as much as it should have at the time.

Who knows exactly what happened to him when he went to war—what he saw in Russia, what he did when he was wounded, what he thought once he came back to his wife after so many months of silence, with so many changes in his body and presumably his spirit. He certainly didn't tell us—but then again, my grandfather didn't speak much. I have vivid memories of spending long summer afternoons following him around as he worked in the field; my sister and I were fascinated by the almost ritualistic quality of his daily tasks, his careful and deliberate gestures, and the odd and amazing tools he used. We desperately wanted to participate, but he never let us, because he wanted to spare us what he believed was hard work, unfit for us, his grandchildren, who were destined for a better life. At the end of the day, he would buy us ice cream and take us home, on his bicycle, one in the back and one in the front. Despite all this, however, I don't remember his voice.

Over the years, I have learned a lot about the conditions in which my grandfather lived. I have found the exact dates for when he left and when he returned. I have discovered some of the places where he went during the war and immediately after it. When I couldn't find any information on his life, "I did my best through other sources from the period and place to discover the world" my grandfather would have seen, as Natalie Zemon Davis did for Martin Guerre and his neighbors. I still don't know how my grandfather felt about his life: whether he cursed his fate or counted himself lucky; what he remembered and what he managed to forget. I don't know if in the end he made some peace with what had happened to him. Yet, I have often thought about all this and have always felt the need to come to some kind of understanding of his life. So I have tried to combine the dates, places, and facts that I do know with the clues I gleaned from observing his quasi-monastic solitude, his silence, his immense unspoken love and pride for my mother—his daughter—and for us, his grandchildren.

I have used this combination of knowledge and conjecture to form as a coherent and meaningful picture of my grandfather as possible. Of course this picture depends, in part, on my proximity to him and is inevitably influenced by my own biases, selective memory, and personal affection. But knowledge and ignorance are present in any historical inquiry, and I don't see that as a reason to give up all attempts to reach a historically sound interpretation.

Lately, I feel that the combination of facts and conjectures I have come up with has taken a somewhat stable and cohesive form, and I can say that I have arrived at a more or less satisfactory account of my grandfather's life. If I manage to find new information, I will need to revise it, and I am sure that as I get older, I will feel differently about it. But right now, by and large, I think I haven't made any glaring mistakes.

My attempt to reconstruct my grandfather's life illustrates my point about trying to stay true to the facts while exercising historical imagination, without blurring the line. And the reason I think this is important is neither to honor my grandfather (after all, he is dead now, and the honors he deserved should have come while he was alive) nor to learn some kind of lesson for the future. One hopes it is unlikely that we will experience an iota of what my grandfather and so many of his generation experienced; moreover, while the story of my grandfather's life could inspire many thoughts about war and its effects on humanity, I doubt that it contains any lessons besides "in case your governors or dictators decide to go to war, try not to be born poor." Rather, constructing this narrative helps me to feel closer to my grandfather while appreciating the differences between his life and mine. It requires that I try to put myself in the shoes of somebody who lived in completely different times and conditions; in order to do that, I must see clearly the distinction between what I know and what I imagine.

The more I think about it, the more I am convinced that the most remarkable value of a history education in the wider world lies not simply in teaching the ability to "think critically," or in providing a set of fairly mysterious (at least to me) "marketable skills" that can magically transform history majors into CEOs of Fortune 500 companies—although I do think that the world of business could benefit from greater attention to the values of a liberal arts education. The main reason that I think history is relevant today well beyond the confines of a university campus lies in the unique ability of history to foster compassion for our fellow human beings insofar as they are both similar to and different from us. Narrative is not the only way, but it is certainly an effective way to communicate this particular kind of historical compassion, based as it is on a combination of knowledge and imagination, proofs and possibilities.

Some readers may find my narrative approach a bit distracting and may be irritated by my liberal use of "perhaps" and "presumably" and by the ease with which I use the conditional as well as (but never in lieu of) the indicative: in this book I often discuss what *might* or *could have happened*, but I never confuse this with what *did in fact happen*. Of course, I respect the reaction of those readers, because I don't claim that my approach is the best or only way to write history, even though I stand behind the decisions I made because I believe they are the right ones for this book. I also know at least a subset of my readers who will appreciate following these stories: my students. As I said at the beginning, I have written this book with them in mind, and much to the delight of Cicero, Quintilian, and indeed all the protagonists of the Western classical and medieval rhetorical tradition, my students are ardent believers in the value of *exempla* as an aid to learning history. I thought they would appreciate my efforts to convey abstract concepts by means of concrete examples.

I also thought this book would be more accessible without the weight of the usual scholarly apparatus. Thus, I have restricted the footnotes to a minimum and have used them only for direct citations from primary sources. Naturally, this book owes much to the scholarship of many other historians, and it is not just a duty but a privilege to acknowledge the works from which I have learned and to point readers in their direction. Thus, at the end of this book I have included a brief summary of bibliographical notes, organized by chapters and arranged thematically rather than alphabetically. These notes are not intended to be complete, let alone exhaustive. Rather, they include only the works on which I have most heavily relied, and which I consider most useful as a starting point for further research.

1

The Making of a Success Story

Carlo Calà was not born into great wealth or an aristocratic family, but by the mid-1650s he had become a fabulously rich and influential officer in the government of Naples. Thanks to a lucrative legal career, a meteoric rise into the upper echelon of the administration, and marriage with a rich and well-connected woman, he amassed enough money to buy himself a fief and, with it, the title of Duke of Diano. The life of Carlo Calà, Duke of Diano, must have appeared to be a story of exemplary success.

The city of Naples was (and still is) stunning for the beauty of its natural surroundings. It was architecturally opulent and culturally vibrant, but also financially overstretched, overcrowded, violent, and very rough around the edges. Naples was capital of the namesake kingdom of Naples, which since 1503 had been part of the Spanish empire. The highest political authority in Naples was the viceroy, who governed the Neapolitan territories as representative of the Spanish sovereign.

Naples was huge: Before the devastating plague of 1656, which killed at least one third, and perhaps as many as half of the urban population, Naples had about 300,000 inhabitants (roughly 10–15 percent of the population of the entire kingdom). This made it the second largest city in Europe after Paris. Most of its inhabitants were immigrants from the provinces, who had come to the city attracted in part by the low price of bread. Once these people made it to Naples, however, they found themselves poor, living in unsanitary conditions, and oppressed by new and ever more burdensome appropriations, which were needed to replenish the perpetually hungry coffers of the Spanish Crown. The silver lining was perhaps

A Fake Saint and the True Church. Stefania Tutino, Oxford University Press. © Oxford University Press 2021. DOI: 10.1093/oso/9780197578803.003.0002

that (if we count Sundays and the months of July and August, when all the days but Thursdays were considered holidays) between religious feasts and political commemorations, the Neapolitans were on holiday about 230 days per year.

This economically and socially difficult situation exploded in 1647, when the Spanish crown increased its fiscal pressure on the kingdom of Naples to support its involvement in the Thirty Years' War. To meet the new demands, the Neapolitan governors issued a novel *gabella* (tax) on fruit. This sparked a riot that quickly spread throughout the city and extended to the periphery of the kingdom. The leader of the revolt was the fishmonger Tommaso Aniello, better known as Masaniello, who was killed shortly after the riots began. The uprising did not end with his death, however, but became an opportunity not only for the poor to protest their conditions, but also for local aristocrats to vent their frustrations. The nobles had always demonstrated a degree of diffidence toward the "foreign" rule of the Spanish viceroy, and they had seen their economic power and their personal wealth progressively diminished, not only because of the taxes and dues they were forced to render to Madrid, but also because of the high cost of living around the viceregal court.

The Spanish found allies in the non-noble elite, of whom Carlo Calà was a perfect specimen. These *togati* (the Italian equivalent of the French *noblesse de robe*) were a relatively heterogeneous group with no ties to the native feudal and municipal nobility. The vast majority of them came from the legal profession. Neapolitans were litigious, and the tribunals of the city were always bustling with activity. Most of the lawsuits concerned matters of inheritance, succession, and alienation of property of the nobility, who needed lawyers and rewarded them handsomely for their services. The legal profession was both respected and remunerative, and it included some men of notable intellectual prowess. These lawyers possessed high social standing, remarkable intellectual capital, and immense personal wealth. The viceroys promoted the Neapolitan *nouveau riche* to the upper echelon of the government and used them as a shield against both the poor and the nobility. Many of the *togati* rose through the ranks of the bureaucracy: they were appointed as judges in the *Gran Corte della Vicaria* (the central civil and criminal court in the city), served as high-ranking officers in the *Camera della Sommaria* (overseeing the fiscal and financial affairs of the kingdom). Several even became members of the Collateral Council, the highest political council advising the viceroy.

This legal and bureaucratic elite should not be imagined as a proto-bourgeoisie or a promoter of a socially and economically progressive agenda against the reactionary "old" nobility. Divided among themselves by many internal conflicts, the Neapolitan *togati* lacked any semblance of class consciousness and had no social or political alternative to oppose to the power and privilege of the nobility. Indeed, the most successful *togati* wanted to mimic the lifestyle and social habits of the nobility, and they quickly and eagerly bought up fiefs, titles, and territorial patrimonies being sold off by impecunious noblemen. The greatest aspiration of a Neapolitan *togato* was not simply to keep up with the aristocratic Joneses, but also to become one of them. He might ennoble himself through marriage, or track down some distinguished ancestor in the family tree to prove that the family had been erroneously excluded from the nobility in the first place. Then the family could be *reintegrata*, or reinstated, among the members of the noble *Seggi* (the administrative wards of the city that included the old families of the urban aristocracy).

This portrait fits Carlo Calà perfectly. He was born in 1617 in Castrovillari, a small town in the deep provinces of the kingdom near Cosenza, in Calabria. He also belonged to a prosperous family of well-connected *togati*. Carlo's maternal uncle, Francesco Merlino, had managed to climb the administrative ladder and become first a judge in the *Vicaria* and then a regent of the Council of Italy in Madrid. This was the body that administered the Italian provinces of the Spanish empire. Upon returning to Naples from

Spain, Merlino was appointed president of the Sacred Royal Council, the highest judicial body in the kingdom of Naples.

Carlo's father, Giovanni Maria, was also a lawyer. Unlike his brother-in-law, Giovanni Maria Calà never made the leap from the province to the metropolis. Thanks to Merlino's support, however, he had become a rather prominent officer in the local bureaucracy and served as the *avvocato fiscale*, or crown attorney, in Cosenza. Giovanni Maria had great ambitions for his son. When Carlo was just six years old, his father sent him to his famous uncle in Naples, hoping that the boy would follow in Merlino's footsteps. Carlo studied law, and after obtaining his degree, in 1639 he entered the firm of Giovanni Andrea di Paolo, a notable lawyer and jurist. Soon Carlo began to make a name for himself as a lawyer, and a good amount of money. Francesco D'Andrea, another seventeenth-century Neapolitan lawyer, jurist, and administrator, worked for a time alongside Carlo in Giovanni Andrea di Paolo's firm. According to D'Andrea, Carlo "dealt with a number of important cases right from the beginning of his career." Whatever Carlo "missed in elo-quence," wrote D'Andrea, "he made up for with his doctrine, good judgment, and dignity." Calà seemed so at ease in the tribunal that "people thought that he was a senior litigator even before he began working."[1]

As successful as he was as a lawyer, however, Calà knew that the legal profession was but a stepping stone to the upper echelon of the administration. Thus, he began attending the meeting of the *Accademia dei Rinforzati*, which was a prestigious and influ-ential association of legal scholars founded by the famous jurist Alessandro Turamini and presided over by Giovanni Andrea di Paolo, Carlo's mentor. Here he honed his skills as a budding govern-ment official. After acquiring a solid body of juridical and political knowledge, Calà started to write his own contributions to support the viceregal government against its enemies.

First, Carlo went after the French sovereigns, who had provided some support to the short-lived Neapolitan Republic after it was proclaimed by the rebels in the aftermath of Masaniello's revolt. In 1648, soon after the rebellion had been suppressed, Carlo wrote a pamphlet under the pseudonym Larcando Laco (an anagram of his own name, as his contemporaries immediately realized). In it he harshly denounced the French involvement in the rebellion against the Spanish Crown as an attempt to "occupy" by violence a kingdom that the Spanish sovereigns ruled "with so many legitimate grounds." According to Calà, the French were nothing but tyrants who "fomented this fancy of a republic in order to destroy the kingdom and make us all slaves," and so "in the kingdom of Naples no freedom and no republic could ever exist under the French."[2] No wonder Masaniello's revolt had miserably failed: "the Neapolitan citizens know full well that their security and peace rests on the ability of the Spanish crown to keep the French out."[3]

Although the viceroys were reasonably successful in keeping the French out, another, and more insidious, enemy of the government could not be so easily thwarted: the Catholic Church. The relationship between the Roman Church and the secular government was a constant source of tension for all sovereigns in Catholic Europe. On the one hand, early modern rulers needed the political and theological legitimation that came from the Vicar of Christ; they used the Catholic religion to impose not just political obedience but also cultural uniformity and social homogeneity on their subjects. On the other hand, in the aftermath of the Reformation and the Council of Trent, early modern popes had assumed an increasingly large role in the political arena as the Roman Church centralized and solidified its theological, religious, and political structure around the institution of the papacy. Not only was the pope an absolute sovereign in his own territory: because of his status as the supreme spiritual leader of all Catholics, he could claim some authority over secular princes themselves, since their consciences, too, were subject to the spiritual authority of the Church.

During the sixteenth and seventeenth centuries, the battle between political and ecclesiastical leaders to strengthen and increase their power regularly flared up both in Italy and abroad. In Naples, the conflict between the Roman Church and the viceregal government hinged on two main issues: criminal jurisdiction and taxes. These were areas in which clergymen traditionally enjoyed special privileges, immunities, and exemptions. As a lawyer and prospective administrator, Carlo Calà understood the high stakes of this juridical, financial, and jurisdictional conflict. Thus, in 1646, he supported the viceroy's pleas by publishing (at his own expense and in his own home) a short text in which he argued that clergymen were not exempt from a number of taxes and regulations issued by the viceregal government.[4]

More specifically, Calà's pamphlet stated that clergymen were not exempt from the custom duties imposed on exporting precious metals, silk, and wheat (whose production and distribution was tightly regulated by the Neapolitan government). They also had to contribute to the maintenance of the roads and bridges. Clergymen were bound to follow the rules imposed by the government on hunting and fishing and had to respect the laws regulating the possession of weapons. Finally, according to Calà, if a clergyman was found to possess a prohibited weapon, he could and should face pecuniary punishment from the secular court.

Calà knew that canonists and theologians would respond that all these duties and punishments were illegitimate because they violated ecclesiastical immunity, specifically as outlined in the papal bull *In coena Domini*. This bull, which had been reissued in 1627 by Pope Urban VIII, included harsh penalties for secular leaders who did not respect the divinely sanctioned privileges and exemptions afforded to ecclesiastical people and properties. For Calà, however, these objections had no merit. First, regardless of any specific privilege or immunity, all clergymen were part of the political community in which they lived, for "they do not cease to be citizens just because of their ordination." Since the secular government issued those fiscal impositions and regulations precisely for the sake of "the common utility" of the community, all the community, clergymen as well as laymen, had the duty to respect them.[5]

Then, moving on to "loftier arguments," Calà wrote that ecclesiastical immunity did not completely exempt clergymen from the jurisdiction of secular authority. While the prince had no right to meddle in spiritual and theological matters, he had the right, and in fact the duty, to rule over the clergy "in all temporal affairs" and in every aspect that concerned "the wellbeing of the commonwealth," which God had entrusted to the prince's care and responsibility.[6] Even influential Catholic theologians such as the Jesuit and Cardinal Robert Bellarmine, Calà wrote, agreed that "insofar as clergymen are citizens and members of the political commonwealth, they are bound to observe the laws of the secular princes" as long as those laws do not rule over spiritual and theological matters. Since the laws issuing new taxes, imposing custom duties, and prohibiting the possession and carry of weapons have nothing to do with the spiritual and theological realm, clergymen must obey them just like any other subject.[7]

Having demonstrated that the clergy cannot invoke special immunity from any purely political law, Calà argued that whenever a clergyman violates any of those laws, he should be subject to the pecuniary punishment of the secular judge. Once again, Calà knew his adversaries would respond that such an argument violated the juridical immunity of the clergy. Nevertheless, he stated that the clergy's juridical immunity referred only to corporeal punishment or jail time, not to pecuniary sanctions. Those, he believed, the political leader could legitimately inflict on any subject, clerical or lay, who was guilty of any crime "against the wellbeing of the community and the common good."[8]

Finally, Calà stated that because *In coena Domini* was never officially published in the kingdom of Naples, its validity was questionable.[9] Even if we assumed that the bull was valid, it did not apply to the cases discussed in his book. In Calà's interpretation, the bull was meant only to safeguard the freedom and immunity

of the Church in its spiritual and religious functions, and to protect clergymen from corporeal punishment. It was never intended
to allow clergymen to commit actions against the commonwealth
or to prevent the secular ruler from punishing them with pecuniary
sanctions.[10]

Although his anti-clerical arguments were not particularly original, Calà stated them with sufficient polemical vigor to provoke
a reaction from both the Roman Curia and the viceregal government. In 1651 the Roman Curia decided to have the Congregation
of the Index of Prohibited Books proceed to an official examination of Calà's text to establish whether it should be included in
the Index among the forbidden books. This was not the first time
that the Congregation dealt with a text arguing against ecclesiastical immunities and privileges in the territories governed by the
Spanish sovereign. Just the year before, the Index had prohibited
a book written by the jurist Francisco de Vico and entitled *Libro
primero de las leyes y pragmaticas reales del reyno de Sardeña*, which
defended the legitimacy of several anti-clerical laws issued in
Sardinia.[11]

When the censors of the Index read Calà's book, they immediately realized that a prohibition was not only warranted but to
a certain extent inevitable. The censors thought that "the author
himself must be expecting this outcome, given that he did not want
to include in his book any approbation, either legitimate or spurious." Furthermore, in the conclusion of his book, Calà explicitly
submitted his work "to the judgment and correction of the Pope";
the censors took this to mean that Calà knowingly "wrote much that
deserved to be censured."[12] On April 10, 1651, the Congregation of
the Index declared Calà's book officially prohibited.[13]

The viceroy, too, took notice of Calà's text. Unlike the Church,
however, he immensely appreciated Calà's defense of the secular government. The viceroy must also have appreciated that by
1648—just as Francesco Merlino, Carlo's famous uncle, was appointed as president of the Sacred Royal Council upon his return

from Madrid—Carlo had written in support of the viceroys not only against the Church but also against the French. Calà's obvious commitment to the viceroy's causes, his seemingly inexhaustible polemical energy, and his impeccable timing (as D'Andrea reported, the ability to write the right things at the right time was Calà's "greatest skill")[14] propelled Calà's meteoric rise through the ranks of the viceregal administration. In 1649, he was appointed crown attorney in Naples, and in 1652, he was promoted to president of the *Regia Camera della Sommaria*. In that same year he married the wealthy and well-connected Giovanna Osorio, a relative of the Marquis of Astorga, who in 1672 would become the new Neapolitan viceroy.

In addition to his notable political and administrative role, by the beginning of the 1650s, Calà had amassed huge wealth. This was thanks to the wealth and properties he had inherited from his parents, the money he had made as a lawyer, the dowry brought by Giovanna, and the compensation from his salary in the administration. As many of his contemporaries attested, Calà was cautious with money to the point of stinginess: "he did not like to throw money around and sought to increase, not waste, his patrimony," which over time became larger and larger.[15]

By the 1650s, it is easy to see why most people in Naples must have regarded Carlo Calà as the perfect model of the self-made man. Coming from a small provincial town (although in a comfortable and socially well-connected family), Carlo had moved to the big city, where he became not only fabulously wealthy and professionally successful, but a mover and shaker in the viceregal government.

But all these accomplishments did not entirely satisfy Calà. There was something else that he (and many other fellow Neapolitan *togati*) desperately wanted: a noble and ancient lineage. Initially he thought that he could buy his way into the nobility; in 1654, he acquired the fief of Diano, in the Southern Apennines, and with it the title of duke, for the considerable sum of 50,000 *ducati*. This roughly corresponds to almost two million dollars in today's money, and as D'Andrea remarked, Calà paid cash without needing "to sell any part of his estate." Yet this recent and store-bought nobility was not distinguished enough for Calà, whose only "vanity" was "to show that his family descended from royal blood."[16]

Carlo Calà's desire for a noble and ancient lineage, and the lengths to which he was willing to go to obtain it, must be considered in the specific context of Naples. Finding evidence of a noble pedigree was not simply a source of pride but could also become a means for the *togati* to achieve the *reintegrazione*, that is, their family's official reinstatement into the noble *Seggi*. As wealthy and influential as the *togati* were, the noble status of *Seggi* conferred social, political, and cultural privileges that only the aristocracy could access.

Carlo Calà and his fellow Neapolitan *togati* were not the only ones in early modern Europe who longed for an ancient and noble ancestor. In the sixteenth and seventeenth centuries, almost any European man who had means and opportunity tried to claim a genealogical pedigree to enhance the nobility of his family. Generally speaking, in pre-modern Europe, novelty was, at best, suspicious, and the concept of authority was tightly linked with that of antiquity. The ability to claim that one's family descended from, say, a medieval emperor, ancient Roman aristocrat, or biblical patriarch provided the economic, political, and social elites a degree of respect and legitimacy that nothing else could provide. Not even Jesus was exempt from this genealogical frenzy. As late as the nineteenth century, the archbishop of Paris Hyacinthe-Louis de Quélen felt the need to point out in one of his sermons that Jesus could boast of an impeccable pedigree: Not only was he the son of God, but he also "came from an excellent family on his mother's side."[17]

It is true that, starting from the late Middle Ages, European society had begun to develop a certain distaste for the concept that nobility rests in the blood, contending instead that the marker of true nobility should be found in the *virtù*, the virtue or character of a person. Nevertheless, linking nobility to virtue did not undermine confidence in the authority of genealogy. First, many of the old ancestors that early modern people were so eager to include in their family trees were notable because of their deeds, so it was their virtue that allowed them to become noble in the first place. Second, antiquity carried its own virtue, and a great one at that. Since ancient people, doctrines, and knowledge were closer to the original and unadulterated stage of civilization (or, from a Christian perspective, closer to the primitive source of the truth of God), they were *ipso facto* authoritative.

All of these intellectual, cultural, political, and theological factors legitimized and encouraged the search for noble, virtuous, and ancient ancestors. Early modern European people had a wide array of potential candidates at their disposal, including medieval and ancient sovereigns, noblemen, and patricians. There were also older and more obscure options, such as those mentioned by the Dominican friar and exemplary forger Annius of Viterbo in the numerous (and in many cases utterly spurious) documents he claimed to have found. In Catholic Europe, however, there was one more potential model: the saint. As a notable ancestor, the saint had a peculiar appeal. Like his or her lay colleagues, the saint is a virtuous and therefore noble person; unlike the others, however, the saint's virtue rests not on natural skills or abilities but on the supernatural charisma bestowed by divine grace. The saint's nobility, in other words, is sanctioned by the judgment not of men but of God.

The city of Naples was a particularly good town for both nobles and saints. Cardinal Alessandro Bichi served as papal nuncio in Naples between 1628 and 1630. At the end of his tenure he wrote a report to the Roman Curia, in which he stated that he found the city of Naples stunning and in fact "rather than simply the head, it might be called the entire body of the kingdom." No other city in Southern Italy had "so many people, so many palaces, and so much beauty."[18] One of the features that most impressed Bichi was "the extraordinary formality and pomp in all exterior things." The Neapolitans immensely valued nobility, and even those who had no titles or money made an effort to dress and behave as if they had both. Bichi found the same love for pomp and luxury "even in the exterior cult of God": Neapolitan churches were "magnificent," and the altars of saints were decorated with "ornaments and apparatus beyond imagination and belief."[19]

Naples was second to no other city in Catholic Europe in its fervor and devotion for saints. By the end of the seventeenth century, Naples had not just one or two but more than thirty patron saints. This number does not include the many unofficial holy men and women who at any given time were said to possess special powers but were never officially canonized by the Church. The official patron saints included traditional choices such as the thirteenth-century Saint Dominic and Saint Thomas Aquinas, as well as more recent saints such as Gaetano di Thiene (the founder of the Theatine order, who died in 1547 and was canonized about a century later) and the Jesuit missionary Francis Xavier (who died in 1552 and was canonized in 1622 alongside Ignatius Loyola, the founder of the Jesuits). Among the Neapolitan patrons were a handful of women (the first female patron saint of Naples was Patricia, a niece of Emperor Constantine), as well as foundational figures in the history of the Church such as John the Baptist. His feast day, held on June 24, saw a spectacular celebration that included one of the largest cavalcades ever to pass through the city, in which even the viceroy participated.

The most famous and celebrated patron saint of Naples was San Gennaro, a semi-mythical bishop of Benevento, a town situated about 30 miles northeast of Naples. He lived under the Roman persecution and was beheaded for his faith in 305 in Pozzuoli, a small town so close to Naples that today it is part of the Neapolitan metropolitan area. By 1497, the relics of the saint had made their way to Naples from the Abbey of Montevergine about 40 miles away. These included San Gennaro's severed skull, some bones, and, most important of all, his blood, which had never rotted and sometimes miraculously liquefied when set before his skull.

San Gennaro's blood did not liquefy every time it was set before his skull. Over time the people of Naples attributed to the liquefaction a kind of prognostic significance, celebrating its occurrence as a sign of prosperity and its non-occurrence as the harbinger of divine punishment. All citizens of Naples, rich and poor, requested San Gennaro's aid in cases ranging from curing infertility and various bodily illnesses to providing a dowry for a daughter; from finding a husband to saving the city from a potentially devastating eruption of Mount Vesuvius (San Gennaro accomplished the latter in a rather spectacular fashion in December 1631). Neapolitan devotees rewarded San Gennaro generously for his help by donating jewelry, money, hand-embroidered altar clothes, and wax (or, in the case of wealthier devotees, silver or gold) statuettes representing the body part that San Gennaro had miraculously cured. In 1614 the records show that San Gennaro received, among other *ex voto* (the Latin name for offerings given to a saint in fulfillment of a vow), about twenty wax statuettes representing hands or feet, ten wax heads, about fifteen silver eyes, and three breasts (one of wax, two of silver).

In addition to the celebrations for San Gennaro and other patrons, the city of Naples saw numerous other religious festivals, processions, and public ceremonies, often involving spectacular apparatuses, lights, and music. Especially notable were the festivities to celebrate the *Corpus Christi* and the frequent celebrations in honor of the Virgin Mary. Naples was chock full of relics: according to a seventeenth-century catalogue, the city possessed more than 360 complete bodies and 50 heads of saints, a handful of thorns from Christ's crown, the blood of Saint John the Baptist, the breast milk of the Virgin, and some of the grease from the grill on which Saint Lawrence was roasted by Roman persecutors in the middle of the third century. Like San Gennaro's blood, many of these relics and other images or statues manifested their supernatural power publicly. The city never failed to mark those occasions with yet another ceremony, such as one held on the day of the Assumption of

Mary (August 15), during which the dried milk of the Virgin Mary also regularly liquefied.

The task of overseeing these devotional and liturgical commitments, and managing the often complicated consequences of such religious fervor, fell to the Neapolitan ecclesiastical hierarchy. It would be wrong, however, to imagine this hierarchy as a relatively compact and harmonious group trying to impose the doctrinal and devotional rules of the post-Reformation Church while fending off occasional jurisdictional attacks by the political government. The Catholic hierarchy in Naples was itself the sum of many parts, often in conflict with one another.

From Carlo Calà's point of view, the most significant aspect of the disagreements within the leadership of the Church was the conflict of interest between the archbishop of Naples and the *ministro,* or representative, of the Roman Inquisition. This conflict was usually latent, but at times it became quite explicit. Before the Holy Office set up its delegated tribunal in Naples, in the 1580s, the archbishop and his episcopal colleagues were responsible for both defending the interests of the Church against the viceregal administration, and investigating and punishing doctrinal deviations and heresy. Because the archbishop and his staff were deeply enmeshed in the local system of social, political, economic, and cultural privileges, the Roman authorities believed that local ecclesiastical leaders were often excessively sensitive to the economic and political pressures coming from the upper echelon of the viceregal court, and thus less than proactive in persecuting the doctrinal crimes of influential people. By contrast, the *ministro* of the Inquisition was a "Roman" agent with no ties to the local power dynamics. This gave him the freedom he needed to investigate crimes without worrying about respecting local privilege or reciprocating local favors.

Tensions between the Holy Office and the local episcopal authorities were not exclusively a Neapolitan phenomenon. Throughout the Italian peninsula we can find evidence of conflicts between bishops and Inquisitors. Nevertheless, in Naples these tensions were more numerous and consequential than in the rest of Italy. This not only rendered the position of the Holy Office in Naples ambiguous with respect to the delicate balance of power between ecclesiastical and secular authorities, but also made governing the Church in Naples a very complicated affair. The relationship between the Neapolitan and the Roman ecclesiastical leaders ranged from cordial and efficient collaboration to open hostility and sabotage.

Carlo Calà was certainly aware that saints played a crucial devotional, political, economic, and symbolic role in the city of Naples. He also knew that the relationship between the Roman Curia and the Neapolitan ecclesiastical hierarchy was not always amicable, because the interests of the Roman Curia did not always align neatly with those of the Neapolitan ecclesiastical leaders. As a good lawyer and able politician, Carlo Calà must have realized that these internal conflicts not only weakened the institutional capital of the Church and its ability to withstand political attacks by the viceregal government, but also undermined the credibility of its local leaders, making them even more vulnerable to manipulation by those who had skills, means, and opportunity.

Given this knowledge, Carlo Calà must have been all the more excited when his desire to ennoble his family tree seemed to be on the verge of fulfillment. Beginning in the early 1650s, several mysterious documents and objects surfaced, seemingly out of nowhere. These contained what appeared to be incontrovertible evidence that Carlo Calà did have a noble ancestor who was not only ancient and glorious but endowed with prodigious spiritual gifts and supernatural powers.

2

A Wonderful Find

Carlo Calà was famous both in the city of Naples and throughout Calabria, the region from which his family hailed and the location of several of his significant property holdings. Especially in the area surrounding the city of Cosenza, everybody knew that the crown attorney Giovanni Maria Calà was a wealthy and, at least at the local level, powerful man, and that his son Carlo was an even more wealthy and influential member of the viceregal government in Naples. Therefore, Cosenza was full of admirers who either were or hoped to become clients, servants, or otherwise close to the Calà. One of those admirers was a man named Ferrante (or, as some sources report, Ferdinando) Stocchi.

Based in Cosenza, Stocchi was a member of the lesser Calabrian nobility. While he was by no means rich, he had sufficient resources to devote himself to a life of the mind. Stocchi had eclectic intellectual interests. He dabbled in poetry and astrology; in 1648 he published a collection of poems entitled *Carmina et lusus*, and in 1655 he wrote a book called *Del portentoso decennio opera astrologica*, in which he predicted the political future of Calabria based on astrological calculations. He was recognized as a leader by the learned community in his town, at one time serving as the president of the local literary *Accademia*. His real passion, however, was local history and antiquarianism, and he believed that his unsurpassed knowledge of local affairs would bring him not only honor among his fellow scholars but also benefits of a more tangible nature.

According to some sources, while strolling through town one day in the late 1640s, Stocchi met Carlo Calà's father. Eager to

A Fake Saint and the True Church. Stefania Tutino, Oxford University Press. © Oxford University Press 2021. DOI: 10.1093/oso/9780197578803.003.0003

impress Giovanni Maria, Stocchi struck up a flattering conversation about the many glorious and famous men who came from, or lived in, Cosenza. Stocchi told Giovanni Maria that he knew of a twelfth-century member of the Calà family named Giovanni Calà. This Giovanni Calà was linked to the German imperial dynasty of the Hohenstaufen, along with his brother Enrico, due to his service in the army of the Holy Roman emperor Henry VI. Even more remarkably, this medieval soldier had at some point left the army to become a hermit, and had received from God the gift of prophecy and other supernatural blessings. On account of this, people venerated him as a saint. Giovanni Maria, who knew how much his son longed for a noble and ancient ancestor, put Stocchi in touch with Carlo some time before 1650 (the year of Giovanni Maria's death).[1]

Carlo must have found Stocchi's news promising, because he responded by giving him money to support more thorough research into the history of his ancestor Giovanni. The duke allegedly paid Stocchi the truly enormous sum of 24,000 *ducati* for his historical and antiquarian expertise. In seventeenth-century Naples, 24,000 *ducati* had a purchasing power of more than three quarters of a million dollars in today's currency; we can imagine how pleased Carlo must have been with Stocchi's research, and how eager Stocchi was to carry out his task.

A few years went by, during which Stocchi continued to dig into the past of the Calà family for information on the mysterious medieval ancestor. By the early 1650s, Stocchi's research had begun to pay off. Stocchi sent to Naples two rare printed biographies of Giovanni that he had discovered. The first had been written by one Martinus Schener and was originally printed in the city of Tiferno (the old name of the town that today is called Città di Castello, in Umbria) in 1473. Schener was supposed to be one of Giovanni's fellow hermits and companions. The second biography was written by Johannes Bonatius, another twelfth-century hermit, and was printed in Autun in 1509.

We can imagine how eagerly Carlo Calà must have read those books, and how ecstatic he must have been when he realized that they not only narrated the amazing life and deeds of his noble and holy medieval ancestor, but also contained "enough clues to find his body." This was allegedly buried in the woods around Castrovillari, a town in the vicinity of Cosenza where Carlo was born. Carlo immediately set out to recover the relics. On May 22, 1654, with the permission of the viceregal court, the assistance of the local bishop, and the presence of "notaries, witnesses, and an immense multitude of people who had come to see the spectacle," he initiated "the search for the valuable treasure" in the Calabrian woods.[2] The search party did not have to work too hard; the following day, they found several bones apparently belonging to a human being of amazingly large dimensions, along with a ball of lead, which contained yet another manuscript narrating the life and deeds of the medieval hermit Giovanni.

In addition to this amazing discovery, in the mid-1650s a great number of manuscripts began to materialize. The majority surfaced in local libraries, personal family archives, and monasteries in the Cosenza area, and a few more were found in Rome, in the Vatican and Angelica libraries. These manuscripts contained further details on the deeds and charisma of the soldier-turned-hermit Giovanni. They were all written in a medieval style of handwriting; their ink and paper appeared to be ancient; and they all referred to Giovanni with the title of *beato*, or "blessed."

From these sources, Carlo Calà was able to acquire a pretty detailed picture of his ancestor. Born around the middle of the twelfth century in Castrovillari, Giovanni was prodigiously tall and big, and while growing up he often displayed extraordinary courage and superhuman strength. Even as a young boy, Giovanni could run faster than the wild boars roaming the woods around Castrovillari. He regularly killed tigers and lions with little more than his bare hands, and on one occasion he threw a ball weighing more than thirty pounds over a distance of a third of a mile.

Giovanni's life as a local giant changed when the Holy Roman emperor Henry VI tapped him and his brother Enrico to serve as captains in the army that he had assembled to conquer the kingdom of Sicily. While Henry had nominally acquired this territory through his marriage with Constance of Hauteville, Constance's nephew Tancred of Lecce—who had ruled over Sicily before his aunt's marriage—refused to submit to Henry's imperial authority, thus forcing the emperor into a war. During Henry VI's campaign in Southern Italy, Giovanni continued to demonstrate his prodigious abilities. One time, alone and on foot, he fought and defeated one hundred enemies on their horses; in another incident he engaged in a duel with ten soldiers, killing them all. During the siege of Salerno, when a giant appeared on the battlefield, Giovanni (a giant himself) cut off the evil giant's head with his sword. The emperor was so impressed by Giovanni's power and skills that he decided to leave Calabria in his hands while the imperial army proceeded southward to Sicily.

Giovanni's brilliant career as a soldier and *de facto* ruler of Calabria came to a premature end when he was severely wounded by not one but three deadly blows. He was miraculously saved by an angel, however, who ordered him to leave everything behind and become a hermit, following in the footsteps of Joachim of Fiore. Joachim, a fellow Calabrian but much better known, was a twelfth-century mystic, theologian, and biblical commentator. Joachim founded the monastic order of San Giovanni in Fiore and, according to his devotees, was endowed with a prophetic spirit and other miraculous powers.[3]

Like that of his more famous contemporary Joachim, Giovanni's life as a hermit was characterized by several supernatural attributes. His fame as a prophet was such that kings and princes routinely came to Calabria to consult with him. His power to perform miracles was also notable. He resuscitated five dead people, including one who had been dead for four days, just like Lazarus, the man whom Jesus was reported to have resuscitated in the Gospel of

John. He single-handedly eliminated the plague, walked on water, and cured innumerable people from various illnesses and diseases, before dying a holy death sometime in the first half of the thirteenth century.

While the discovery of Giovanni's extraordinary life must have made his seventeenth-century successor very happy, it also created some potential problems. To begin with, seventeenth-century Italy was not exactly a welcoming place for prospective saints. The Protestants were already attacking the superstitious nature of the Catholic cult of saints, and the pope wanted to impose his centralizing authority over local and episcopal ecclesiastical leaders. As a result, the Roman Curia had begun to discourage the proliferation of local cults to ensure that the process of saint-making was tightly controlled by the Roman center. In 1588 Pope Sixtus V instituted a new Papal Congregation, called the Congregation of Rites and Ceremonies, which was charged with overseeing all cases of canonizations. As the sixteenth and seventeenth centuries progressed, the Papal Curia took more decisive steps to regulate and standardize the criteria for being recognized as a saint. Pope Urban VIII was especially active in this process: during his pontificate, the Curia firmed up the requirements for sanctity, instituted a juridically strict procedure to apply for canonization, and granted to the Congregation of Rites and Ceremonies the authority to issue the final sentence.

Even as Urban VIII's policies gave the Roman center unprecedented power in matters of saints and miracles, the papacy recognized that it would have to tread lightly with local cults. As we saw in the case of San Gennaro, a significant amount of political power, civic pride, and socio-economic benefits depended on the veneration of local holy people. The papacy did not want local ecclesiastical authorities to indulge indiscriminately the people's belief in "saints" who had received no official stamp of approval from Rome, but it also realized that some form of compromise was necessary. Pope Urban VIII understood this delicate equilibrium very well. He forbade any form of public veneration to someone who had not been formally canonized, but agreed to make an exception in the case of any saint whose cult had not been fully ratified in Rome but could be shown to be *ab immemorabili,* that is, to have existed from time immemorial.

In a series of decrees issued by the Holy Office between 1625 and 1634, the pope allowed the publication of books praising the deeds of these local and as yet unofficial holy people, on two conditions. First, the books would need to contain a disclaimer or *protestatio* stating that any supernatural or miraculous deed attributed to the protagonist had not yet been officially approved by the authority of the Church; readers should grant to these miraculous narratives the same credibility that any human narrative warranted. Second, the content of the book was to be thoroughly reviewed and approved by local bishops as well as by the Holy See.

In addition, by the end of the sixteenth century, post-Reformation Catholicism had begun to embrace the methods of philological and historical criticism introduced and practiced by the Humanists. Over the course of the seventeenth century, ecclesiastical scholars (like their secular colleagues) were using increasingly sophisticated tools to analyze, date, and authenticate documentary evidence. This newly critical attitude was especially evident in discerning the truth of sanctity. Before Luther and before the spread of textual analysis, judging the truth of sanctity mostly meant discovering whether the supposed saint acted under the influence of God as opposed to that of the devil. Afterward, judging the truth of sanctity became as much a matter of evidence as of faith. The Roman leaders were supposed to find out not only whether the saint in question acted under divine or demonic influence, but also whether the supposed saint's deeds actually happened. Further, their deeds had to be the manifestation of an authentic supernatural charisma instead of the result of an overactive imagination, deception, or forgery.

The relationship between the truth of Catholic doctrine and the authenticity of its sources, however, was far from simple. Catholic historians and scholars sought to discover the historical and documentary truth about saints and miracles with a distinctive urgency, because they knew that the purity of the Catholic faith was at stake. Catholic leaders were more invested than anybody in making sure that the true and universal Church of Rome rested on the solid pillars of historical authenticity. Consequently, early modern Catholic historians (as well as their Protestant counterparts) not only adopted the tools and techniques that enabled them to distinguish the authentic from the fake, but also made important contributions to the development of the modern historical method.

Applying philological and textual criticism to sacred history and hagiography, however, sometimes produced results that challenged the theological and exegetical tradition of the Catholic Church. Digging deep into history could surface utterly uncomfortable truths, as happened when Lorenzo Valla demonstrated that the Donation of Constantine—the document that recorded the Roman emperor Constantine's decision to give the pope political and spiritual authority over Rome and the Western empire—was a forgery. As more and more scholars of all religious confessions agreed with Valla, it became increasingly clear that the document was fake. Catholic leaders knew that crucial theological, and not just historical, traditions of the Church were predicated on the authenticity of the Donation.

Some Catholic theologians feared the theological, exegetical, and polemical consequences of admitting that the document was a forgery. They decided that the best course of action was to reaffirm their commitment to the document's authenticity and to ignore or discard all contrary evidence. Other Catholic intellectuals felt that the historical and textual proofs of forgery were too numerous to be discredited; these individuals accepted that the document was not authentic and tried to adjust the theological account of the relationship between Christianity and the Roman Empire accordingly. Either way, it is clear that many people in Rome realized the importance of historical authenticity, not only for the past but also for the future of the Catholic Church. They were fully aware how difficult it could be to juggle the truth of history with the truth of doctrine.

These early modern Catholic historians and scholars were exercising a critical attitude in a cultural, religious, and theological context in which the miraculous, properly identified and understood, was an inherent part of the supernatural. In their world, the miraculous was not only real but also drastically different from the incredible. The incredible was man-made, feigned, and false; it was dangerous precisely because it could jeopardize belief in the miraculous. The miraculous was eminently credible (and, if regulated appropriately, necessary for salvation) because it was a direct emanation of the divine. Therefore it did not belong to the realm of nature and could not be tested or verified using the same tools and techniques that were used to authenticate human documents.

Catholic theologians, historians, and scholars who were asked to evaluate the truth of sanctity faced a complex situation. Thanks to their knowledge of documentary criticism and textual analysis, many could distinguish quite confidently (if not always correctly) the fake from the authentic. Nevertheless, they also knew that "authentic" was not a synonym of "true," because not all manifestations of truth could be authenticated by means of human reason or skill. Authenticating a document on the life of an alleged holy person did not prove that the person was holy; conversely, not being able to authenticate a holy person's deed did not exclude the possibility that the deed was miraculous.

Carlo Calà must have anticipated that his recently discovered ancestor would face an uphill battle to sainthood. First, Giovanni was one of many local holy people on whom the Roman Curia was trying to crack down. Second, he was both literally and metaphorically larger than life. Because Giovanni's life and deeds exceeded the natural limit of human abilities in so many ways, Carlo could expect that the Curia would go over his case with a fine-tooth comb. Finally, up until the middle of the seventeenth century, there seemed to have been no popular devotion to Giovanni, and therefore no way for Carlo to claim that his ancestor's cult existed from time immemorial. There was no record of Giovanni's very existence in any medieval secular or ecclesiastical chronicle. The fact that Giovanni had burst onto the scene so suddenly and seemingly out of the blue would certainly have raised the already high level of critical and documentary scrutiny to which the seventeenth-century Curia was subjecting all cases of prospective sanctity.

Despite these hurdles, however, the Duke of Diano was not discouraged. The appearance of Giovanni, an extraordinarily strong and brave soldier whom the Holy Roman emperor had trusted with governing Calabria, provided incontrovertible evidence of the ancient aristocratic lineage that Carlo had always wanted. Giovanni was not only noble and heroic but also a holy man and prophet, with a substantial number of miracles to his name. He seemed to possess all the required characteristics to be publicly venerated and officially canonized.

Carlo also believed that the local power dynamics were in his favor. Giovanni's holiness could not but be seen with great admiration by the Catholic hierarchy, whose relationship with the Neapolitan administration was often far from amicable. After so many unpleasant conflicts over taxes and juridical immunity between the Catholic hierarchy and the viceregal government, Carlo was sure that the Catholic leaders would rejoice to see a protagonist member of the Neapolitan administration promoting and fostering the people's devotion to the Church and its most venerable members. They would certainly embrace this opportunity to include Giovanni Calà among the official saints of the Church.

Reassured by these considerations, Carlo Calà rolled up his sleeves and got to work on promoting his ancestor. First, like any good early modern lawyer, Carlo made sure that every document, artifact, or relic concerning Giovanni was officially recorded. To this end, he saw to it that the local bishops in Calabria, as well as the archbishop of Naples, then Cardinal Ascanio Filomarino, were involved in the search for Giovanni's remains, and that witnesses appointed on their behalf were present when the bones were discovered. Then Carlo solemnly donated the sacred relics to a local monastery so that they could be appropriately preserved. In addition, he ordered that all the manuscripts that had emerged in libraries and monasteries in Rome and throughout the kingdom of Naples be copied in the presence of public notaries and official witnesses, and that a copy of every document be stored in the public archive. In this manner, the manuscripts relating the hitherto unknown story of Giovanni ceased to be simply historical sources in need of scholarly verification, and became official public documents or *instrumenta*, that is, formal notarial records. Having these manuscripts transcribed and put on record as publicly authenticated documents gave them the seal of political and legal (if not necessarily historical and scholarly) authenticity. In this way, Carlo thought, they would become acceptable legal proofs of his ancient lineage and pivotal tools in his campaign to convince the Neapolitan municipal leaders to reinstate the Calà family among the traditional aristocratic *Seggi* of the city.

Carlo was not just a skilled lawyer but also a shrewd politician. He knew that registering the documents as official archival records would not be enough to ensure the success of his plan. Giovanni's claim to fame rested not merely on his military prowess and his short-lived career as the *de facto* ruler of Calabria, but more particularly on his hitherto-unknown status as a saint. Giovanni was not dynastically linked to the emperor, and since his religious calling had led him to quit the secular world, he had no heirs to whom he might have transferred any political power the emperor might had granted him. For these reasons, Carlo realized that he needed to produce an accurate genealogy that would link his name more solidly with Giovanni's, and to promote Giovanni's sanctity through official ecclesiastical channels.

To accomplish this goal, Carlo first decided to write a history of his family, focusing on the life and deeds of his remarkable ancestor. The resulting work, entitled *Historia de' Svevi,* was a historical treatise that straddled the boundaries between sacred and profane. Carlo told his readers that the treatise was written "in the style of the lawyers," and therefore they should not expect to find "elegant prose," "erudite orations," and "hyperbolic exaggerations," but rather "rigorous examinations" of "incontrovertibly authoritative" documents found "in libraries and archives."[4] Carlo realized that the aim of this "rigorous examination" was mainly to glorify his own family, but he also knew that he was following in the footsteps of famous men who had written celebrated genealogies of their own and their patrons' families. In addition, the protagonist of Carlo's genealogy was not just an average nobleman, but a saint. Carlo explicitly stated that his main motivation for writing the book was his "desire to clarify whatever might be useful for the canonization process" of his ancestor. Insofar as Carlo's work was not only a genealogy but a hagiography, his models included not just secular writers but also "holy Fathers," both ancient and modern, who "glorified the holy Apostolic See" by recording for posterity the miraculous deeds of the most remarkable members of the Church.[5]

Carlo divided his *Historia* into three sections; Giovanni was the central protagonist of the first two. The first section introduced the historical context in which Giovanni lived; it discussed Giovanni's secular life, describing both the prodigious strength that Giovanni exhibited as a young boy and the courage and bravery he demonstrated while serving in the emperor's army. The second section focused on Giovanni's religious life, providing a detailed account of all the prophecies and miracles he performed while living as a hermit. Carlo enriched his narrative by reproducing substantial sections of the newly found printed and manuscript material. These "incontrovertibly authoritative" documents that he had entered on record would guarantee the truthfulness and authenticity of his account.

The final section was the genealogical part of the treatise. In it Carlo reconstructed the entire family tree, starting with Giovanni and his brother Enrico (who had married twice and had four children) and ending with Carlo himself. Carlo was especially proud of his genealogical research. He had uncovered not only numerous missing links between himself and the medieval Calà brothers, but also some evidence that his family deserved to be reintegrated among the Neapolitan aristocratic *Seggi*. When the Hohenstaufen dynasty lost control of Southern Italy after the death of Frederick II, the descendants of Giovanni's brother Enrico had moved to Naples. There, according to some sources, the local aristocracy recognized their distinguished status by including them in the *Seggio* of Capuana, which had many members and enjoyed a distinctive prestige among the other *Seggi*. Over time, the original membership of the Calà family in the *Seggio* of Capuana had been forgotten. Carlo was sure that his new evidence, coupled with the prestige of having a saint in the family tree, would convince the Neapolitan aristocracy that it was time to rectify this old mistake and restore the seal of ancient nobility to the Calà family.

The only hurdle left was to convince the Roman Curia that Giovanni was indeed a saint. As we know, this was not an easy task. Carlo must have been familiar with the standards and procedures imposed on any prospective saint by the Roman Curia; he was certainly aware of the complex relationship between the religious and political interests of the Roman Curia and those of the Neapolitan ecclesiastical hierarchy. Thus, he devised a multipronged and wide-reaching propaganda campaign to work this situation to his benefit.

As soon as he completed his *Historia*, Carlo obtained a printing license from the viceregal government. But because the treatise contained a hagiography of Giovanni and was composed as an aid to canonization, Carlo knew that a license from the political government would not satisfy the Catholic censors. In order for the Catholic hierarchy to allow its publication and circulation, the *Historia* would need to comply with papal laws regulating the publication of such works. Pope Urban VIII's decrees concerning unofficial holy people whose cult had not existed from time immemorial included the following rules: books relating their deeds must be thoroughly vetted before being printed, and they must contain a *protestatio* explaining that any miracle or supernatural gift narrated in the book had not been officially approved and thus was solely the product of the author's own opinion. To meet this requirement, Carlo added a disclaimer to his treatise. This stated that although Carlo's sources attested to an ancient cult and veneration of Giovanni's divine charisma, Giovanni's saintly status had not been yet approved by the Church; therefore readers should consider the book's information simply as the fruit of the author's historical research. At that point, Carlo gave a copy of the treatise (with the disclaimer) to the archbishop of Naples, Cardinal Filomarino. The cardinal appointed a *revisor*, or reviewer, to check the text and make sure it did not contain anything that challenged Catholic doctrine and morality. After the archbishop received the green light from his reviewer, he granted Carlo permission to publish the book.

With the government's license and the archbishop's permission in hand, Carlo set out to select a publisher for his book. Seeking to strengthen his relationship with local Neapolitan ecclesiastical authorities (and thus to exercise additional pressure on the Roman Curia), Carlo reached out to Novello de Bonis. Bonis had become the official printer of the archiepiscopal court when his predecessor Francesco Savio died during the 1656 plague. In the space of a few years, Bonis had acquired quite a reputation in Naples as an innovative and audacious printer; he had published books narrating the deeds not only of officially canonized saints but also of holy people who had strong credentials for future canonization. For instance, Bonis effectively discovered and launched the career of the Jesuit author Antonio Barone, who published a number of hagiographies of recently deceased Southern Italian Jesuit fathers. Among them were the writer and educator Antonio Pavone and the ascetic and self-mortifying father Evangelista de Gattis; they had not been officially proclaimed saints, but their lives (so their followers and companions claimed) had been characterized by a special divine inspiration. When Bonis saw Carlo's book, he must have been intrigued by the tale of the soldier-turned-holy-hermit, and he could not pass up this opportunity to stay ahead of the hagiographical curve. Bonis printed Carlo's *Historia de' Svevi* in 1660.

Carlo's *Historia* had received the official approbation of the local archbishop and was being produced by the official printer of the archiepiscopal court. Yet these endorsements did not guarantee that Giovanni's case would be favorably received by the Roman Curia. A conflict over Giovanni's saintly status would not have been the first case in which Neapolitan and Roman ecclesiastical leaders found themselves on different pages. Because the process of saint-making was tightly controlled by the Curia, Carlo knew that the support of local ecclesiastical leaders would not be sufficient—he would need to get the Roman Curia on board.

The problem was that Carlo's track record with the Roman Curia in general, and with the Roman censors in particular, was not exactly positive. In the 1640s, when Carlo was desperately trying to get the viceregal administration to notice him, he had participated in the jurisdictional conflict between the Neapolitan viceroy and the Roman Curia. More specifically, in 1646 Carlo wrote and self-published a book entitled *De contrabannis clericorum,* arguing that clergymen living in the kingdom of Naples were subject to the fiscal and jurisdictional authority of the viceroy. While Carlo's strategy paid off with the Neapolitan government, it provoked a reaction from the censors of Congregation of the Index, who in 1651 officially prohibited Carlo's text. Carlo realized that the 1651 incident might come back to haunt him if the Congregation of the Index were harboring any resentment; the censors might be more likely to scrutinize the *Historia* for doctrinal errors. Carlo needed to find a way to make amends with Rome and return to the Curia's good grace.

Luckily, Mount Vesuvius lent Carlo a helping hand.

3

An Unexpected Ally

On July 2, 1660, Mount Vesuvius began to spew smoke, fire, and ashes. A few days later, Monsignor Giulio Spinola, papal nuncio in Naples at that time, reported to his Roman superiors that "the volcano continues to vomit balls of fire, and even though the lava does not seem to advance, nevertheless the fire is more and more frightening." Although the eruption had not yet caused the death of many people, "the smoke and ashes extend up to the Amalfi coast, and the lands on the slopes of the mountain are irreparably destroyed."[1] The inhabitants of Naples braced for what they feared would be a disaster of immense proportions. That had happened with the 1631 eruption, and its memory must still have been vivid. About a week after the eruption began, however, the volcano quieted down, and the people breathed a collective sigh of relief. But this was not the end of the story. In the middle of August, about a month after Vesuvius ceased to erupt and the city was still dealing with a massive amount of ash, an unsettling phenomenon started to manifest.

At the beginning of September, Monsignor Spinola told the Papal Curia that "a few days ago, a rumor started to spread that after the eruption of the Vesuvius, the people living in the countryside next to the volcano had begun to see crosses appearing on their linens." Some of the crosses "were black, others red, and it was impossible to wash them away." Initially, the nuncio did not relate the news to Rome because he believed that "it was just gossip." Yet seeing that the rumor continued, he had sent some people to inquire on the matter. The nuncio's eyewitnesses reported that the appearance of the crosses was "very true," and they had personally seen crosses not only on people's linen bedding and clothing but also on altar cloths

A Fake Saint and the True Church. Stefania Tutino, Oxford University Press. © Oxford University Press 2021. DOI: 10.1093/oso/9780197578803.003.0004

in neighboring parish churches. One of the nuncio's agents counted "twenty-seven crosses on one altar cloth alone." In the meantime, the nuncio learned that some religious orders were already on the case, and "the fathers of the Society of Jesus had already sent some samples" of the linens "to their Provincial superior." Finally, the nuncio reported that Neapolitan citizens were becoming agitated because they feared that the crosses were an "evil omen." The papal diplomat was now convinced that the phenomenon of the crosses had to be taken seriously, and he asked his Roman superiors for advice on how to proceed.[2]

The Roman leaders urged the nuncio to check with the archbishop of Naples and see what he knew about the mysterious crosses. The nuncio immediately complied, and reported back that the archbishop of Naples had also heard of the strange phenomenon and had begun his own investigation. The archbishop had asked a parish priest in his diocese to deliver him a sample of linen with the cross-shaped stains. Once he had obtained it, he had it washed over and over again. He found that "even though those holy signs could not be completely cancelled, nevertheless their black color had started to fade." The archbishop also told the nuncio that some people, terrified by the potentially evil implications of these events, had asked him to hold some kind of public ceremony "to placate God's wrath." While the archbishop personally had no interest in spreading more anxiety within his flock over this alleged manifestation of God's anger, the nuncio reported, "if the Viceroy makes a specific request to this effect he is ready to comply, because he does not want to be accused of neglecting to assuage the fear of the people, who are already exhausted by such a string of recent calamities."[3]

The situation was becoming difficult to manage. As Neapolitans grew more and more agitated, the local political and ecclesiastical leaders were torn between different needs. On the one hand, both the archbishop and the viceroy thought it wiser to downplay the appearance of the crosses, because a frightened mob could cause riots and public disturbances. On the other hand, neither the viceroy nor the archbishop wanted to be perceived as careless in this matter. If people demanded that their leaders propitiate the divine favor, they felt they had no choice but to comply.

In the meantime, crosses continued to appear throughout Naples and the surrounding areas, and "investigating the possible causes" had become "the biggest source of curiosity in the city of Naples." Most people interpreted the crosses as some kind of "evil prediction" for the future of the city and its inhabitants, and even some priests in their homilies explained them as a sign of "imminent catastrophes and calamities coming from God." Other priests were more level-headed, reminding parishioners that "the sign of the holy cross could never be a bad omen." Among those moderate voices was that of one Jesuit preacher at the Church of the *Gesù Nuovo*. The nuncio was pleased that this preacher "encouraged the people not to panic" but rather "to trust that God's divine mercy would save them from any misfortune."[4]

A small minority of Neapolitan citizens looked for causes other than God's wrath, and in particular "some medical doctors say that those crosses are the entirely natural effect of some specific vapors emanating from Mount Vesuvius and depositing over linens." Others responded that this explanation did not hold, because "the crosses are of several different shades of red and black," and the same substance could not have "so many different effects." Besides, many of the crosses had appeared "not only on the linens hanging outside to dry, but also on those kept inside chests of drawers." How could vapors emanating from the volcano reach so deep inside these containers?[5]

Seeing how widely the phenomenon was spreading and how deeply it affected all sorts of people—preachers, medical doctors, poor farmers, the upper echelons of the government—the archbishop of Naples realized that the mysterious crosses had the potential to undermine the political and religious stability of the city. Therefore, he decided to involve the Inquisition. From Rome, the cardinals of the Holy Office ordered both the archbishop and the *ministro* of the Neapolitan tribunal of the Inquisition to perform two tasks: first, investigate the phenomenon further to make sure it was not a "scam," and second, calm the Neapolitan people, reminding them that rather than acting out their fear of potential calamities, "this was a perfect opportunity to give themselves over to God from the bottom of their heart."[6]

The local ecclesiastical leaders immediately went to work on the first item of the Inquisitors' agenda. Over the next few weeks, the archbishop, the nuncio, and the *ministro* gathered as much information as possible from local bishops throughout the Neapolitan diocese and neighboring parishes. The picture emerging from these local reports shows a range of credulity, concerns, and responses. The bishop of Nola reported that he had personally seen many examples of crosses "especially on the sleeves of blouses and on altar clothes"; he knew that many people in his diocese thought those crosses were divine signs. In his experience, however, many of the crosses seemed to "disappear completely" with multiple and vigorous washes. Thus, as far as he was concerned, there was no "certain or true evidence" of any supernatural origin.[7]

The bishop of Castellammare took the crosses more seriously. In mid-September 1660, he reported a number of sightings of crosses on linen, and while some of them disappeared after washing, others did not. He pointed out that he had done some research on the phenomenon, and while he had no doubt that this was in fact a "God-sent prodigy," he did not feel equipped to "understand either its cause or its effect." He was happy to leave this task to his superiors, endowed with the necessary "prudence and doctrine."[8]

Despite this realization of his shortcomings, however, the bishop was not ready to abandon his investigations. A couple of weeks after this letter, he wrote again to his Roman superiors to alert them "of a most curious fact." The abbess and several nuns living in the Carmelite convent of Santa Maria della Pace told him that "a small cross had appeared on the thigh of a servant." With the best bucolic metaphors he could muster, the bishop reported that initially the cross was "of the color of a ripe bitter orange," and after "several attempts to wash it off with soap," the cross had not disappeared, even though it had changed to "the color of the peel of a pomegranate."[9]

By the beginning of October, sightings of crosses were being reported not just around Naples but in the distant peripheries of the kingdom, far from the reach of volcanic ashes. Several "processions and other ceremonies were being set up out of fear for the calamities that might befall."[10] This worried the Neapolitan leaders immensely, and the nuncio learned that "this week the Cardinal Archbishop of Naples had a private conversation with the Viceroy, and they did not speak about anything other than those crosses."[11]

In this difficult situation, the Neapolitan leaders turned to the second item on the Holy Office's agenda: calming the people and channeling potentially dangerous panic into controlled, well-regulated, and orderly devotion. One of the best ways to do this was to control and manage public opinion by censoring the books and pamphlets dealing with the crosses. Despite their conflicts, the political and religious leaders collaborated quite closely in this endeavor, seeing how useful it could be for all of them. In late October 1660, the nuncio informed the Roman Curia that the Neapolitan government had received from "an astrologer" a request for permission to publish "a rather long astronomical text" discussing the significance of the crosses. The nuncio was pleased to report that after reading it, the viceroy "found it full of ominous predictions, such as general pestilences, civil wars, death of kings and other calamities," and therefore he refused permission to print it "so as not to frighten the people."[12]

In addition to censoring unsuitable texts, the Catholic hierarchy in both Naples and Rome did what it could to foster the dissemination of pious and reassuring interpretations of the phenomenon. The famous and influential polymath and Jesuit professor Athanasius Kircher set to work immediately to publish his own take on the crosses, which promised to be just what the Curia needed.

By 1660, Kircher already had a rather extensive knowledge of Mount Vesuvius and of volcanoes in general. In the 1630s, he had personally observed the eruption of Mount Etna and had climbed to the top of Mount Vesuvius, exploring and inspecting its crater and summit. Volcanic activities were a crucial subject of the large and influential treatise about the earth that Kircher was then writing; this was entitled *Mundus Subterraneus* and came out in 1665. Kircher's familiarity with Vesuvius and his insatiable curiosity about any novel and mysterious phenomena might explain the speed with which he threw himself into analyzing the appearance of the crosses. By the beginning of October 1660, as new sightings and details were still being reported, Kircher had already completed a manuscript to submit to the Jesuit censors for approbation.

Kircher's text, entitled *Diatribe de prodigiosis crucibus*, was an attempt to use science to calm the people and simultaneously invite them to repent and submit themselves to God and the Church. The book's main argument was that the crosses were not a sign of God's anger but rather a manifestation of nature's amazing properties. Kircher believed that Vesuvius, like all other volcanoes, contained within its depths several minerals: Vitriol (sulfates) and natron (a carbonate and sodium mixture) in particular were expelled during the eruption. Because the 1660 eruption happened in the heat of summer, Kircher reasoned, the sun had transformed these expelled minerals into vapors. By the time Kircher completed his manuscript, people had reported sightings of crosses only on textiles made out of linen. Kircher explained this by arguing that once the volcanic vapors were deposited on linen, they condensed and coagulated following the folds and creases of the fabric, thus creating the shape of the cross. When the vapors fell on wool or silk or other fabrics that did not present the distinctive crisscross pattern of linen, the vaporized substances were absorbed homogeneously, without taking any distinctive shape.

When the censors of the Society of Jesus saw the manuscript, they were perplexed. They knew that the Roman Curia wanted to avoid spreading panic and must have appreciated the reassuring tone of Kircher's explanation. Nevertheless, they thought Kircher's book was problematic. The censors took issue with what they thought was Kircher's excessive insistence on the natural character of the phenomenon. Since the Roman Curia wanted to encourage people to use the appearance of the crosses to rekindle their devotion to the Church, the censors thought that Kircher's interpretation of them as a "merely natural effect" might foster skepticism and draw people away from the Church.

At the same time, the censors complained that Kircher's natural explanation fell short on its scientific merits. The Jesuit censors (among whom was Honoré Fabri, a relatively prominent seventeenth-century natural philosopher) noted that Kircher's argument rested on the specific characteristic of linen fabric, which accounted for the cross-like shape created by vaporized substances. The problem was that over the course of the fall of 1660, the crosses had started to appear not only on linens but also "on fruit and even on human flesh," as the bishop of Castellammare attested after seeing the leg of a servant in the Carmelite convent. This was incontrovertible evidence that Kircher's hypothesis was not correct. The censors feared that if they allowed the book to be printed as it stood, "learned people might actually laugh at it," and the reputation of both Kircher and the Society would suffer a terrible blow. Perhaps, the censors thought, the reason for Kircher's mistake was the haste with which he had written his text. Rather than publishing an evidently flawed work, they believed that Kircher should first take the time to "get a complete and truthful understanding" of the phenomenon.[13]

Aside from the specific merits or flaws of Kircher's book on the crosses, the censors knew that Kircher was a famous and well-respected author. They realized that the leadership of the Society of Jesus might not be willing to prohibit the manuscript and thus anger an important protagonist of the Catholic world of learning. Also, the situation in Naples was growing more and more fraught, and Catholic leaders felt a sense of urgency to cool rising tempers. Evidently aware of this, the censors concluded their report by indicating that they might be willing to let Kircher publish his book provided that he made some modifications. Kircher listened to the censors' comments and implemented the majority of them, though he did not change the main argument and structure of his text. His *Diatribe de prodigiosis crucibus* was eventually published in 1661, with the Jesuit General's permission.[14]

Carlo Calà watched closely as this situation unfolded. Given his position in the upper echelon of the viceregal government, he was privy to the discussions and concerns of the Neapolitan leaders. He must have thought that if he could find a way to help defuse the panic created by the crosses while encouraging people's devotion to the Church, he would be both contributing to the political tranquility and stability of the kingdom, and putting himself into the good graces of the Roman Curia. In 1661, Carlo published his own treatise on the crosses, entitled *Memorie storiche dell'apparizione delle croci prodigiose*. It was written in Italian and printed by Novello de Bonis, the printer of the archiepiscopal court who had published Carlo's genealogical history the year before.

After a relatively brief historical overview of past appearances of crosses and their possible explanations, Carlo's *Memorie* demonstrated that eruptions were not just natural events but manifestations of God's anger toward the sins of his people. As Carlo put it, Mount Vesuvius might very well "contain by nature what it needs to ignite its fire," but nature alone is not the cause of its ignitions. Unlike Kircher, Carlo did not provide any detailed scientific explanation of the phenomenon. Rather than wasting time with science, his readers should assume that whenever Mount Vesuvius erupts, it is acting "as a minister of God's divine justice."[15] Since the 1660 crosses started appearing as a consequence of the eruption, their origin was equally divine and supernatural.

Nevertheless, Carlo admitted that "it is not possible to establish with certainty which specific message from heaven these crosses actually convey." In this situation, Carlo concluded, there was no point in being frightened by a calamity that might or might not occur. "The best remedy to overcome fear and invigorate one's heart is to look at those prodigies with humility and devotion," repent of one's sins, and follow the Church. If people did all of these things, they could be sure that God's anger would be placated and that the crosses would bring nothing but "consolation and grace."[16]

The main thesis of Carlo Calà's book was not that different from Kircher's. Both Carlo and Kircher conceded that volcanoes contained by nature all the elements needed to precipitate an eruption and its consequences, including the formation of crosses. The fact that nature had provided Vesuvius with the necessary ingredients to erupt did not necessarily mean that God's will was not at play, since all natural events, including dramatic and uncommon ones like a volcanic eruption, are part of God's plan. Finally, both admitted that since it is not possible to ascribe any specific supernatural meaning to the crosses, the best way to react was to commit oneself to God and the Church. The main difference between their texts was one of emphasis: whereas Kircher sought to highlight the natural chain of events that must occur in order for the crosses to appear, Carlo emphasized the divine will that was ultimately responsible for setting those events in motion.

This difference in emphasis was all the more striking if we think of the different political, religious, and intellectual roles that Calà and Kircher occupied. Since Kircher was a leading member of the Society of Jesus as well as a famous and respected protagonist of the learned culture of his time, Kircher's book would have been read as the official statement from the Jesuit and Catholic intelligentsia on the phenomenon of the crosses. Carlo Calà, by contrast, was a lawyer and administrator with few or no credentials in learned circles, and his relationship with the Roman Curia had thus far been rocky. Clearly the Catholic leaders expected more from

Kircher than from Carlo, so the bar was much higher for Kircher's book. For this reason, the two books enjoyed very different receptions from the Catholic hierarchy. The Jesuit leaders doubted that Kircher's Latin book was either pious enough to stir people toward the Church, or rigorous enough to command admiration and respect among the learned. Carlo Calà's book, written in Italian and thus aimed at a wider but also more local and less specialized readership, came out with the ringing endorsement of the archbishop of Naples and enthusiastic approbation by the Neapolitan Jesuit theologian Scipione Paolucci.

In the end, neither Carlo nor Kircher had the kind of impact on people's credulity and devotion that they had hoped to achieve. By the time their books came out, nature (or divine providence) had already taken care of business on its own. After reaching their peak in late October of 1660, in a matter of weeks the crosses began to disappear as mysteriously as they had appeared. By the beginning of December, no new sighting had been reported, and as the cross-shaped stains began to fade from linens, fruits, and people's limbs, so too did the Neapolitan people's anxiety. In the middle of December 1660, the nuncio was happy to report that life had gone back to normal in the city. Whatever anger God might have harbored against Naples seemed to have been dispelled, given that during the regular December ceremony of the liquefaction of San Gennaro's blood, "people were so happy to see that the miracle had occurred and that the blood had liquefied."[17]

Even though the prodigy of the crosses did not last long enough to have significant consequences, it brought several benefits to Carlo Calà. Besides enabling him to make a good impression (*fare una bella figura*, as a Neapolitan aristocrat would have said) on the Roman Curia, the crosses provided him with a potentially useful ally in his multi-pronged propaganda campaign for his medieval ancestor and potential saint Giovanni. When Carlo realized that the famous Athanasius Kircher had written a book on the same subject, he decided to use their common interest in Mount Vesuvius as an excuse to reach out to the Jesuit professor and enlist his help in Giovanni's cause.

Between the end of 1661 and the middle of the 1660s, Carlo Calà wrote to Kircher frequently to compliment him on his intellectual standing. Carlo considered this to be "higher than any other man that ever lived in Christendom,"[18] and congratulated him for "the greatness of your doctrine and wit" in discussing "most sublime and deep subjects."[19] Carlo also offered to do some work on Kircher's behalf. For instance, Carlo acted as a go-between between Kircher and other Neapolitan intellectuals and theologians such as Juan Caramuel, to whom Carlo passed on Kircher's letters and books. Carlo also promised to assist the Neapolitan Jesuit college in its administrative conflicts with the viceregal administration. He enthusiastically agreed to take time out of his busy schedule, which required him to deal with "the most important affairs of the kingdom," to deliver a copy of Kircher's *Mundus Subterraneus* to the confessor of the Queen of Spain by means of his contacts with leading members of the Spanish crown.[20]

What Carlo wanted in return was to stir Kircher's interest in his ancestor Giovanni. He hoped that, when the time came, Kircher would support his case for Giovanni's canonization by the Roman Curia. Carlo knew that in the early 1660s Kircher was writing his *magnum opus,* the already quoted *Mundus Subterraneus.* He also knew that a section of this work was supposed to discuss the bones of giants that could be found buried under the earth. Carlo was thus quite happy to alert Kircher to the existence of his ancestor Giovanni, a fine specimen of a giant, whose bones Carlo had dug up from the woods of Calabria. Moreover, during Carlo's research on his ancestor, he had come across a manuscript work by the Augustinian friar and local historian Luca Mandelli. Since the manuscript "contained many things concerning giants, and more specifically evidence that giants seemed to have existed in the kingdom of Naples even in recent times," Carlo was happy to pass the manuscript on to Kircher.[21] In addition to the material pertaining to Giovanni and other giants, Carlo sent a copy of a few documents concerning his medieval ancestor and asked Kircher for help in interpreting "the true and authentic meaning" of some inscriptions and medallions that Carlo had uncovered.[22]

Kircher gracefully (though not entirely unselfishly, given the favors that Carlo had offered) agreed to help clarify the meaning of the documents concerning Giovanni. He even mentioned Giovanni Calà as a medieval giant in the final printed edition of the *Mundus Subterraneus*. As Kircher introduced the topic of fossilized bones in that book, he wrote that "it is possible to find several documents mentioning the finding of skeletons of immense magnitude." As an example, Kircher referred to the recent discovery of the bones of Giovanni Calà. This discovery, Kircher wrote, had been described by the "most excellent and erudite Duke of Diano," "verified by the testimony of the Viceroy," and "confirmed" by the writing of Luca Mandelli.[23]

In his subsequent discussion of the topic, Kircher was not as kind to giants as Carlo might have wished. After conceding that the existence of buried bones of giants had been attested by several sources, Kircher went on to demonstrate that they were highly unlikely to belong to human giants. First of all, Kircher reasoned that given their density and composition, human bones could not support a truly gigantic body—it would collapse under its own weight. Even assuming that such humongous people could exist, how would they find a place large enough to live? "How much food would they need to eat?" For people so big, Kircher estimated that "an entire herd of sheep or goats would hardly be enough for a daily meal, and a bull hardly sufficient for a snack." When these giants were thirsty, they would "no doubt drain entire springs and rivers," not to mention the problem of clothing themselves. "The sails we use in boats would be nothing but a small garland" for such a big creature, and if a human giant "were to use sails for clothes, he would need fifty of them all sewn up together."[24]

In conclusion, Kircher admitted that the Bible explicitly mentions antediluvian giants. Since he would never dare to question the truth of Scripture, he was happy to concede that before the Flood, giants might very well have roamed the earth. Nevertheless, he thought that the time of the giants had probably ended at that point. Whatever giant bones could be found today either belonged to elephants or other massive animals, or were not bones at all but fossilized rocks that "nature formed to look like bones."[25]

Despite Kircher's skepticism regarding recent giants, Carlo Calà must have been happy to find his name and that of his ancestor Giovanni in the published masterpiece of such a well-known author. Carlo received his copy of the *Mundus Subterraneus* in the spring of 1666, and immediately afterward he wrote to Kircher. Though he hadn't read the book yet, Carlo was impressed by its size: It was "the largest and most voluminous" of the books that Kircher had written thus far, and Carlo "could not wait" to find the time to read it carefully and enjoy the fruits of such a "venerable and marvelous author."[26] About a month later, when Carlo had finally read the *Mundus Subterraneus*, he complimented Kircher for "a stupendous and admirable work." Even though Carlo knew that all of Kircher's texts "had been immensely praised by everybody," he anticipated that this new book would encounter even more "success and admiration" among readers.[27]

By the middle of the 1660s, then, Carlo had good reason to be satisfied with the progress of his propaganda campaign. He must have felt that he had made the most of Giovanni's relics and the extraordinary number of sources related to his life and deeds. Carlo had made sure that the ecclesiastical authorities were fully involved in the finding and storing of the relics, and he had systematically registered all the textual documents and sources as official notarial records. He had written a substantial book (published by the official printer of the archiepiscopal court) not only narrating Giovanni's amazing deeds but also demonstrating the genealogical ties linking Carlo's family to that of the soldier-turned-hermit.

In addition, Carlo had taken full advantage of his insider know-ledge of the power dynamics between the viceregal government and the Neapolitan Church to write a timely and pious explanation of the prodigious crosses. This strengthened his position in the eyes of the local ecclesiastical leaders and provided the opportunity to forge a bond with Athanasius Kircher. Carlo hoped that all these elements would convince the Roman Curia that, despite his earlier anticlerical positions, he remained a devout, well-connected, and well-respected member of the Church. This benevolence, Carlo believed, would greatly increase the chances that the Catholic leaders would welcome Giovanni Calà among the official saints.

There remained one last action for Carlo to take in support of his ancestor Giovanni's cause. All of the sources and manuscripts that Carlo had found explicitly described Giovanni as a follower and companion of Joachim of Fiore. Joachim was much more famous than Giovanni but had not been officially canonized, and many people in Calabria were putting pressure on the Roman Curia to give Joachim the honor and veneration they thought he deserved. Carlo believed that tying together the campaigns to canonize Joachim and Giovanni would be beneficial to both candidates. Thus, Carlo set to work on the Joachim front as well, hoping that if events continued in the way he wanted, the people of Calabria would soon celebrate the canonization of not one but two of their most deserving compatriots.

4

A Controversial Partner

Giovanni Calà burst onto the scene suddenly and seemingly out of nowhere. Joachim of Fiore, Giovanni's supposed inspirator and companion, had long been a presence in the religious, spiritual, and liturgical landscape of the kingdom of Naples, and especially in Calabria, the home of the Calà family.

Joachim was born around 1135 in the Cosenza area, where his father was a notary, probably working in the service of the archbishop of Cosenza. Initially, Joachim followed in his father's footsteps and held a bureaucratic appointment at the court of William I, king of Sicily. In 1167, while in the king's service, Joachim went to Constantinople. From there he continued to the Holy Land, where he felt a special calling from God to abandon his lay life and devote himself to religion. Upon returning from Palestine, Joachim decided to join the Cistercian monastery of Corazzo in his native Calabria, and in 1177 he was elected abbot. Eventually, however, Joachim decided that the duties of a Cistercian abbot did not allow the time he needed for reading, writing, and contemplation. After taking a rather long and productive sabbatical and asking permission of the pope, Joachim abandoned Corazzo. In 1190 he founded his own monastic community in the isolated town of San Giovanni in Fiore, deep in the Sila mountains in northern Calabria. In 1196, Pope Celestine III officially approved the rule of Joachim's new monastic order, which was in effect a stricter branch of the Cistercians. A few years later, in 1202, Joachim died.

Over the centuries, Joachim's fame spread. Many of his devotees revered him as an influential and original theologian and biblical interpreter, as well as a holy man endowed with several

A Fake Saint and the True Church. Stefania Tutino, Oxford University Press. © Oxford University Press 2021. DOI: 10.1093/oso/9780197578803.003.0005

supernatural gifts, most notably as a seer. Not everybody was a fan, however. Some theologians and ecclesiastical leaders praised the sophistication of Joachim's method of interpreting Scripture and the far-reaching and insightful consequences of his distinctive view of history. Others believed he had pushed his visionary theories far past the point of doctrinal and scriptural orthodoxy.

For instance, at the Fourth Lateran Council, in 1215, Pope Innocent III officially condemned one of Joachim's texts (now apparently lost), entitled *De unitate et essentia Trinitatis*. In it Joachim allegedly accused Peter Lombard, one of the most celebrated medieval theologians, of having misunderstood the essence of the Trinity. A few decades later, in 1255, Pope Alexander IV condemned as heretical the so-called theory of the Eternal Evangel (or Everlasting Gospel), which the Franciscan monk Gerard of Borgo San Donnino had developed from Joachim's eschatology. Although Joachim was never condemned as a heretic and the vast majority of his texts remained free from censure, these episodes significantly marred his reputation. In fact, Joachim is one of the few Catholic theologians (if not the only one) to appear in several Catholic collections of saints and blessed people as well as in several Catholic catalogues of heretics.

In addition to the controversies that some of Joachim's theological doctrines provoked, his prophecies did not always come true. Sometimes they even got him into trouble. For instance, at the end of 1190 he was summoned to Sicily by the king of England, Richard I the Lionheart. Richard was en route to fight in the Third Crusade and wanted an audience with the famous monk and prophet before battling the infidels. During their meeting, Joachim predicted a big victory for the king, foreseeing that his army would recapture Jerusalem (which did not happen). After hearing the good news, Richard asked Joachim what he thought about the Antichrist, and Joachim allegedly responded that the Antichrist had already been born and was living in Rome. The king (and many people later on) believed Joachim was referring to the pope. Needless to say, this reference to the "Roman Antichrist" was not exactly prudent; several theologians and ecclesiastical leaders over the centuries used this as evidence that Joachim was not only a false prophet but a heretical enemy of the papacy.

Sometimes, however, Joachim's prophecies were correct. Luckily for him, one of these instances occurred at a politically crucial juncture and resulted in some much-needed aid to Joachim and his followers. Readers are already familiar with the military campaign organized by the Holy Roman emperor Henry VI against his nephew Tancred of Lecce to conquer Southern Italy —this was the occasion on which the emperor allegedly noticed Giovanni Calà's superhuman strength and abilities. Joachim followed that battle closely, and not simply out of concern for the political stability of Southern Italy. Tancred had donated a rather large amount of money to Joachim's monastic community, and Joachim was understandably concerned for the future of his patron. In 1191, Henry VI laid siege to the city of Naples, and when the Neapolitan citizens refused to surrender, he ordered his troops to escalate the violence. Joachim went to Naples to try to reason with the emperor. The Calabrian monk told Henry that the siege of Naples could be read as a parallel to the siege of Tyrus by Nebuchadrezzar, king of Babylon, as narrated in the Book of Ezekiel. Since the king of Babylon conquered Tyrus in the end, Joachim told Henry that the victory of the imperial army was inevitable; therefore there was no need to keep committing atrocities. Impressed by Joachim's prophecy, Henry VI ordered his troops to abandon the city of Naples. When the emperor succeeded in conquering Southern Italy following the death of Tancred, he repaid the favor by granting several concessions and privileges to Joachim and his monks. These included a perpetual income of fifty gold bezants to Joachim's monastery in San Giovanni in Fiore.

This income, while not astronomical, was still quite decent. It is difficult to reconstruct the exact value of a gold bezant in Joachim's time, but as a ballpark figure we should consider that in the twelfth century, an Italian merchant was said to have paid the extravagant sum of 10,000 bezants so that his nephew could marry Cécile Dorel, heir to some highly coveted coastal lands on the eastern shores of the Mediterranean. On a more mundane level, in medieval England one gold bezant was enough to buy one cow, or three pigs, or about 150 chickens.

Once again, the mixed results of Joachim's predictions resulted in wildly different assessments of his prophetic charisma. Many influential Catholic theologians, historians, and intellectuals thought that Joachim was not only a dangerous theologian but also a veritable fraud when it came to prophecy. Perhaps the most damning judgment of Joachim's prophetic abilities came from Cesare Baronio, the greatest historian of post-Reformation Catholicism, who openly called Joachim a "fake prophet."[1]

Fortunately for Joachim, others disagreed with Baronio and believed that Joachim's predictions were but one of many supernatural gifts he had received from God. Unsurprisingly, among Joachim's most animated advocates were the members of his own monastic order. They kept the memory of their holy founder alive and, in the middle of the fourteenth century, officially asked the Roman Curia to begin the formal procedure for canonization. The Roman Curia did not proceed with the canonization immediately, and over time, the number of members of Joachim's order dwindled. By 1570, the few remaining monks obtained permission from the pope to be reincorporated back into the Cistercians. Despite the extinction of his order, however, Joachim's devotees in Calabria remained fervent in their zeal and never lost hope of seeing their patron officially included among the saints of the Church. In 2001, eight centuries after Joachim's death, the archbishop of Cosenza initiated yet another request to Rome to open an official canonization procedure, which has not been brought to a conclusion to this day.

Outside of the relatively restricted circle of local devotees, many others felt the allure of Joachim over the centuries. In the

seventeenth century, Joachim received the rather unexpected endorsement of the Jesuit Daniel Papebroch. Papebroch was the
leader of a team of ecclesiastical historians and scholars (called
Bollandists after the group's founder, the Jesuit scholar Jean
Bolland), whose task was to compile and publish a definitive and
historically accurate catalogue of all the Catholic saints: the so-
called *Acta Sanctorum*. The Bollandists' research was based on a
rigorous and extensive documentary and philological examination
and was conducted with the utmost respect for historical authenticity. Given the Bollandists' scrupulousness and high scholarly
standards, many people were surprised that Papebroch inserted a
long entry devoted to Joachim in the seventh volume of the *Acta
Sanctorum,* which included biographies of all saints and blessed
people whose feast day was celebrated in May. Papebroch called
Joachim "blessed" despite the fact that the Curia had not yet given
him any official title.[2]

Papebroch's passionate endorsement of Joachim's charisma
was rather self-interested: Papebroch believed that Joachim had
predicted the foundation of Papebroch's own order, the Jesuits, and
seemed to endow them with a crucial spiritual role in the history
of humanity. Yet the Bollandists' support was still a major boost for
Joachim's local devotees in Calabria and throughout the kingdom
of Naples. Over the course of the seventeenth century, even the political leaders of the kingdom of Naples, both at a local and at the
central level, began patronizing Joachim's case. They believed that
having one of their subjects officially canonized would be a spectacular public-relations coup that would greatly increase their authority and prestige in the eyes of the people.

In sum, by the middle of the seventeenth century, it looked as if
the stars had finally aligned and were shining bright over Joachim.
Neapolitan and Calabrian leaders, both secular and religious,
sponsored and facilitated the efforts of Joachim's followers to put the
medieval prophet at the center of the Roman Curia's map. Between
the end of the sixteenth and the beginning of the seventeenth

centuries, several Cistercian monks residing in the monastery of San Giovanni in Fiore or nearby had begun collecting and copying manuscripts related to Joachim's life and deeds, in anticipation of his canonization. Most important among these manuscripts was a biography written by Joachim's companion Luca (who served as archbishop of Cosenza between 1203 and 1224), as well as accounts of several miracles that Joachim was supposed to have performed both in life and after death.

Some of this manuscript material was used in a biography of Joachim written by the Cistercian monk Giacomo Greco, entitled *Ioacchim Abbatis et Florensis Ordinis Chronologia*. This was published in Cosenza in 1612 and dedicated to the archbishop of Martirano, the diocese that included the monastery in Corazzo, where Joachim had served as abbot. While Greco's work had the merit of refreshing the Calabrian people's memory concerning Joachim and his order, Greco was remarkably restrained about Joachim's supernatural charisma. Greco knew that the Curia had not yet started a formal procedure to canonize Joachim, and he did not deem it appropriate to dwell too much on his miracles before the Curia opened an official case. Instead, Greco sought to provide simply a "chronological account" of the life of Joachim and the history of his religious order, based only "on incontrovertible documents" and leaving aside all manuscript material that could not be historically verified.[3]

A substantial portion of the manuscripts, including those that related miracles that Greco had decided not to use, ended up in the hands of Camillo Tutini, a Neapolitan antiquarian and student of ecclesiastical history. He in turn passed them on to his friend Ferdinando Ughelli, a Cistercian monk and ecclesiastical historian. Ughelli was the author of a massive nine-volume treatise entitled *Italia Sacra*, which provided a comprehensive history of all mainland Italian bishoprics. Ughelli used the manuscripts "of my erudite friend Camillo Tutini" in the section of his work describing the diocese of Cosenza.[4] At the beginning of that section, he briefly mentioned Joachim, stating that he was "endowed with the spirit of divine *intelligentia*" and "left several books of prophecies." Ughelli admitted that some of the writings attributed to Joachim were "suspect of heresy," but he was confident that Joachim's views were fully orthodox and his "reputation for sanctity" fully justified.[5]

Ughelli's *Italia Sacra*, published between 1644 and 1662, was a highly influential work, widely considered to be the official history of the Italian bishoprics. In the decades after the publication of the last volumes, many local ecclesiastical historians took inspiration from Ughelli's treatise to write a historical account of their own local churches and parishes. Realizing the importance of Ughelli's work, several popes tried to have it updated and revised. Joachim's followers must have been pleased to see that Ughelli had seemingly endorsed Joachim's sanctity, because this would make it clear to the Roman Curia that Joachim's name was circulating outside of Calabria and in the larger Catholic world. Nevertheless, because of the nature of his work, Ughelli could not provide the full hagiographical account that Joachim's supporters thought was necessary to give the final push to the canonization. This is exactly what a Calabrian Cistercian abbot by the name of Gregorio de Laude (or de Lauro) set out to do.

Gregorio de Laude was born in 1614 in Castrovillari, the same Calabrian town as Carlo Calà, Duke of Diano (as well as Carlo's ancestor, Giovanni), from a family belonging to the lesser local aristocracy. After completing his novitiate in the Cistercian monastery of Corazzo, Gregorio took his vows and was ordained in 1638. Soon afterward, Gregorio left Calabria to go to the Jesuit college in Naples and then to the Roman College to finish his theological studies. Once he obtained his degree, Gregorio went back to Calabria, and in 1650 he was appointed abbot of the Cistercian monastery of Santa Maria in Sagittario.

Gregorio was fond of history because he firmly believed that collecting historical documents and passing them on for the benefit of posterity was the best way to honor his religious calling. Gregorio was also relatively knowledgeable about documentary research. While Gregorio was in Rome to complete his studies, he befriended his confrere Ferdinando Ughelli, and in the following years he occasionally helped Ughelli to prepare the *Italia Sacra*. For example, during his tenure as abbot of Sagittario, Gregorio uncovered several documents in the local archives in and around the monastery. He used these sources to compile the annals of the monastery, including a list of all abbots who had served since the foundation of the monastery in the twelfth century, and sent all of these materials to Ughelli to aid him in his research on the diocese of Cosenza.[6]

Besides contributing to Ughelli's *Italia Sacra*, Gregorio had a historical project of his own. He believed that Joachim of Fiore was not only a local Calabrian hero but one of the most glorious products of the Cistercian order. Thus the time had come for Joachim to be canonized and honored as he deserved. Gregorio set out to write the definitive hagiographical account of Joachim's life and deeds, demonstrating Joachim's undeniable supernatural gifts and dispelling once and for all the rumors that still circulated about the unorthodoxy of his thought. Ughelli paid back his debt of gratitude by passing on the collection of manuscripts pertaining to Joachim that had been assembled by Camillo Tutini. These served as the documentary backbone of Gregorio's hagiography.

Ughelli was not the only person who knew of Gregorio's project on Joachim and was willing to share his documentary findings. Carlo Calà had also learned that Gregorio was writing about Joachim, and he too had sources that he thought could be useful. We do not know how Gregorio and Calà first met. Both were natives of the same small town, and it is possible that the duke was informed of Gregorio's interest in Joachim by some common local acquaintance. It is also possible that Gregorio met his illustrious fellow townsman in Naples, during his time at the Jesuit college. Regardless of how they became acquainted, it is easy to imagine the reason behind their collaboration. Given his ambition of providing the ultimate hagiography of Joachim, Gregorio was understandably eager to get his hands on all possible sources. Calà, with his un-canny ability to sense which way the political wind was blowing, must have realized that the canonization of Joachim would satisfy the needs of several different political and religious constituencies. Joachim's inclusion among the saints was closer than it had ever been. Carlo decided that this was a perfect opportunity for his an-cestor Giovanni to jump onto Joachim's bandwagon. Giovanni had allegedly been a follower of Joachim in life—why not follow him in posthumous glory and honor as well? For these reasons, Carlo Calà passed on to Gregorio all the printed sources and manuscripts documents that Stocchi had given him, which narrated in great detail the deeds and miraculous prophecies of Giovanni Calà, Joachim's relatively obscure, but no less charismatic, fellow hermit and prophet.

By the end of the 1650s, Gregorio de Laude had completed his book, which amounted to an unapologetic defense of Joachim's sanctity against all naysayers past and present. For Gregorio, Joachim was not only a shining example of Christian virtues and a divinely inspired Biblical interpreter; he was also the author of sev-eral miracles and prophecies, attesting to the special favor that God had bestowed upon him.

Gregorio had no patience with those who criticized Joachim's theological views as bordering on heretical. All the works that had been verified to have been written by Joachim attested to the fact that his views were fully "Catholic." Any other interpreta-tion was to be attributed to Joachim's "evil and ignorant enemies," who had "distorted" Joachim's thought.[7] Gregorio had even less patience for those who, like Baronio, believed that Joachim was not a true prophet; for Gregorio, Baronio and his supporters had misunderstood the actual sense of Joachim's predictions, and therefore had quite simply made a "mistake" in need of being "corrected."[8]

As evidence of the divine nature of Joachim's prophetic gift, Gregorio added to his biography a long section that reported and explained all the prophecies Joachim had made concerning the popes. These would demonstrate that Joachim's predictions had always been accurate, whether they concerned good popes such as the "pious and holy" Celestine V, or evil popes such as Boniface VIII, whose papacy, as Joachim correctly foresaw, was characterized by "immense depravity," "greed," "arrogance," and "unbridled ambition."[9]

Gregorio was evidently aware that his biography could serve as a fundamental repository of evidence for Joachim's canonization trial, which he hoped would be initiated in the near future. Accordingly he dutifully dotted the i's and crossed the t's of his manuscript by making sure that it complied with Urban VIII's decrees regarding the publication of hagiographical material about holy people who had not yet been canonized. First, Gregorio stated that Joachim's case was not subject to the papal rule that prohibited the veneration of men and women who had not been officially proclaimed saints or blessed by the Church. The cult around Joachim had lasted for "many centuries," and thus qualified as dating from time immemorial. Gregorio admitted that his book reported numerous "miracles and prophecies" that had been attributed to Joachim by "several illustrious authors" and not yet been formally approved as such by the Apostolic See. Consequently, he added a disclaimer specifying that these accounts were the fruit of the author's own historical research, and thus that readers should give them no more credence than they would to "any other human history."[10]

When Carlo Calà saw Gregorio's book, he must have been pleased to see the good use Gregorio had made of Carlo's manuscripts and sources. Gregorio had assigned Giovanni quite a prominent place in the story, making him the protagonist of two substantial chapters. In the first, Gregorio introduced Giovanni as a "hermit of distinguished nobility and immense sanctity," telling the story of his military prowess, splendid political career, and divinely inspired decision to leave all worldly honors to follow in Joachim's footsteps. He also related several of Giovanni's miracles, prophecies, and visions.[11] In the other chapter, Gregorio discussed the "friendship" between Joachim and Giovanni, reported the text of a few letters between the hermits, narrated more of Giovanni's miracles, and resolved a few chronological discrepancies that he had identified in the sources.[12]

Besides spreading the story of Giovanni, Gregorio did Carlo Calà another favor by including in his book a veritable cover blurb for Carlo's own upcoming work. When discussing the sources attesting to Giovanni's miraculous deeds, Gregorio told his readers that if they wanted to know more about Joachim's friend, they should know that "the most illustrious, masterly erudite and knowledgeable Carlo Calà Duke of Diano" had written at length about Giovanni "in his book *Historia de' Svevi*, which, God willing, will soon be published."[13]

By 1656, a draft of Gregorio's book had received the approbation of the local ecclesiastical authorities in Cosenza, but the book was not published there. It is very likely that Carlo Calà, recognizing the importance of Gregorio's book not just for Joachim's case but for Giovanni's, used his contacts in the entourage of the archbishop of Naples to allow Gregorio to publish his book in a more prestigious venue. In December 1659, Gregorio's book was submitted to the archbishop of Naples for approval, and in January 1660, the archbishop's reviewers gave it the green light for publication. Gregorio's book was printed by Novello de Bonis, the official printer of the archiepiscopal court, in 1660—the same year in which he published Carlo's *Historia de' Svevi*.[14]

We can imagine Carlo's great expectations at that point. Both his book and Gregorio's had been published with the approbation of Neapolitan ecclesiastical leaders and by a much respected printer, ensuring both works a wide circulation. Joachim's stock had never been higher, and his canonization had never seemed more within reach. Carlo must have been convinced that his ancestor Giovanni had everything to gain and nothing to lose from his association with Joachim, which had been confirmed by so many documents and explored by two different books. Now Carlo had only to sit and wait for the Roman Curia's reaction to these two Calabrian saintly men.

Unfortunately, the Roman Curia did not seem particularly interested in Carlo's book. In 1660, nobody in Rome had ever heard of Giovanni Calà, and one can understand their lack of interest in a book written in Italian about a relatively obscure episode of medieval history featuring an utterly unknown protagonist. Joachim of Fiore, however, was a different story. Joachim was famous and famously controversial; the Roman hierarchy was aware of the hostility that Joachim provoked in some circles, and the veneration and respect he commanded in others. The Roman censors realized that Gregorio's hagiography was likely to be considered the definitive historical account of Joachim's deeds and the ultimate theological defense of his claims to sanctity.

Nevertheless, a quick read of the text revealed a few potential problems. Gregorio liberally lauded Joachim as "a blessed, saint, and divine prophet" even if the Curia had never officially proclaimed Joachim as such. Moreover, Gregorio did not refrain from "bad-mouthing" and "railing against" Joachim's detractors, including venerable figures such as Cesare Baronio and Pope Innocent III. Finally, Gregorio mentioned "one Calabrian prophet" who, despite being completely unknown by the Curia, allegedly shared Joachim's "spiritual intelligence" and ability to "predict the future."[15] For these reasons, at the beginning of March 1661, the Secretary of the Congregation of the Index "presented" Gregorio's book to his colleagues for a detailed and official examination.[16]

From the records we have, we know that the censors decided to concentrate on only three, relatively minor, faults with Gregorio's book, all dealing less with content than with tone and style. First, the censors felt that Gregorio had written "irreverently" about Baronio and other authors who had criticized Joachim.[17] Second, Gregorio had been much too aggressive in his defense of Joachim's theology, especially when he stated that it was "certain" that those who criticized or condemned it were "evil and ignorant enemies" of Joachim.[18] Finally, the censors did not appreciate Gregorio's less-than-flattering descriptions of several medieval popes, especially Boniface VIII, whom Gregorio, interpreting Joachim's prophecy, had branded as "greedy," "arrogant," "ambitious," and "depraved."[19]

The censors did not engage in depth with the authenticity of Gregorio's story. Their task was to make sure that the book contained nothing against Catholic doctrine and morality, not to launch a full historical and documentary investigation of the truth of the historical facts. Moreover, while they realized that the book's main goal was to demonstrate that Joachim received from God the supernatural ability to perform miracles and predict the future, they also knew that demonstrating the truth of such divine inspiration was different from proving the authenticity of a historical occurrence. Miracles and prophecies are such precisely because they defy all possibilities of human verification. Besides, the task of establishing whether a Catholic person was truly a saint fell on the Congregation of Rites and Ceremonies. The Congregation of the Index dealt with books, not with canonization trials, and therefore the only duty of the censors was to decide whether the book was consonant with Catholic theology and piety.

Despite all these qualifications, however, at least one of the censors, Orazio Quaranta, manifested anxiety over the truth of the facts. Quaranta, a former Jesuit who had translated Teresa of Ávila's epistles into Italian, remarked that Gregorio's book contained many things that "smelled like fiction." Quaranta singled out the "miracles and prophecies he [Gregorio] attributes to one Giovanni Calà, a former soldier turned hermit."[20] In Quaranta's opinion, even if Gregorio tempered his judgment on Baronio, revised his account of the background to Joachim's condemnation by Innocent III, and toned down his description of Boniface VIII, many "meaningless, fake, and indeed apocryphal" passages would still remain in the book. Quaranta knew that pointing out and correcting the meaningless, the fake, and the apocryphal was outside of his purview as a censor for the Index, but he closed his censure wishing that "after so many centuries of discussion, the case of Joachim would be trusted to the opinion and judgment of people not only more honest and pious, but also more intelligent and learned."[21]

Quaranta's wish fell on deaf ears. As he himself admitted, the censor's job was to identify the unorthodox, not the fake, and aside from the problems already mentioned, the censors found no serious fault with the book's Catholic doctrine and morality. Moreover, in compliance with Pope Urban VIII's decree, Gregorio had added a disclaimer that Joachim had not yet been canonized by Rome. His narrative of Joachim's holy and miraculous deeds was to be considered simply the fruit of his own research, not the Church's official endorsement of Joachim's status as a saint. If it turned out that Gregorio's account of Joachim's charisma was based on fake sources and apocryphal texts, the author alone, not the Church, would bear the responsibility. For all of these reasons, the censors decided that Gregorio's book did not deserve absolute prohibition. They suspended it *donec corrigatur* ("until corrected"), providing the author the opportunity to correct the mistakes and issue a new, fully approved, edition.[22]

In January of 1664, Gregorio asked the Index to provide him with a list of the corrections they wanted to see.[23] The members of the Index wrote down their requests, which were relatively minimal. They wanted Gregorio to speak more "benevolently" about Baronio, to explain that Joachim was "probably" rather than "certainly" condemned because of his enemies' influence, and to delete all the insulting adjectives Gregorio had used to describe Pope Boniface VIII.[24]

In February of 1664, the Congregation approved the printing of a corrected version. As far as I know, no new edition of this book was ever published, possibly because Gregorio had died in the meantime.[25] Nevertheless, many people found out that Gregorio's hagiography had passed the scrutiny of the Index with only minor official corrections. One of these people was the Bollandist Daniel

Papebroch. At the beginning of his entry on Joachim in the *Acta Sanctorum*, Papebroch told his readers that his goal was to demonstrate that Joachim's fame for sanctity was fully justified. To do this, Papebroch had relied heavily on the historical information and documentary sources in Gregorio's book. Papebroch knew that the book had been "suspended" until corrected, and since no new corrected edition had come out, he was using a book that had been officially condemned by the Congregation. Nevertheless, the condemnation was "light" (*leviter*, which was the mildest form of condemnation for both books and people, as supposed to the harsher degrees of *vehementer* and *violenter*). Besides, Papebroch was using the book simply as a "historical account," and thus without endorsing any theological or moral doctrine that the Index might have found worthy of condemnation.[26] After this disclaimer, Papebroch used Gregorio's biography extensively throughout his entry on Joachim, borrowing not simply facts and sources but also the arguments that Gregorio had used to defend Joachim from detractors.

Carlo Calà also noticed that Gregorio's book had emerged from the scrutiny of the Index relatively unscathed. Most likely, Carlo was unaware of Quaranta's report, in which the censor explicitly mentioned the chapters on Giovanni Calà as examples of numerous "fake" and "apocryphal" parts of the book that "smelled like fiction" (Quaranta's report was exclusively destined for internal discussion, and it is improbable that a copy had been leaked outside of the Congregation). Even if Carlo's contacts in the upper echelon of the Neapolitan secular and religious administration had alerted him to Quaranta's reservations about Giovanni's story, Carlo would have been relieved to know that no other censor shared Quaranta's concerns, which were not mentioned in the official list of corrections given to Gregorio.

These considerations must have convinced Carlo Calà that the time had come for Joachim to be crowned among the saints, and consequently for his own ancestor Giovanni to receive the honor and veneration he deserved. Thus, Carlo upgraded his printing campaign to spread Giovanni's fame. To circulate the story of Giovanni among a wider circle of readers, he decided to enlarge his Italian book *Historia de' Svevi* and translate it into Latin as *De gestis Svevorum*. In addition to changing the language, in this new version of the book Carlo gave Giovanni a more prominent role. To that end, he greatly reduced the sections illustrating the genealogical tree of the Calà family and divided the work into two volumes, devoted to the secular and religious phases of Giovanni's life. Most of the work was composed of virtually complete editions of many of the recently found medieval manuscript and printed sources, together with Calà's short commentaries or introductions.

By the end of 1663, the work was ready for the press, and Carlo initiated the process of obtaining the required permissions from both the Neapolitan archbishop and the Neapolitan government. He did not know that by that time, his prospects for success had taken a sharp turn for the worse.

5

The Fraud Is Uncovered

By this point, I am sure the readers of this book have judged the story of Giovanni Calà and his supernatural powers to be entirely implausible. They might be surprised to learn that anybody in seventeenth-century Naples or Rome would give the slightest measure of credibility to the story, which defied both human reason and the laws of nature. Such readers might conclude that Carlo Calà's contemporaries were very credulous indeed. After all, a society that so readily believes in miracles, prophecies, God-sent post-volcanic crosses, and other such occurrences that cannot be proved either by reason or by experience must hold a much looser standard for credibility than does our modern society.

Those who agree with these statements are in very distinguished company. In the entry devoted to the verb "to believe" in the *Encyclopédie*, Denis Diderot wrote that not all acts of belief are equally commendable. If we believe in something after having "examined the matter well," and having made a proper use of our reason, then our belief will be "solid and satisfied." If we believe without a reasonable examination, Diderot wrote, we have "sinned against our own reason" and "neglected the most important prerogative of humanity" because we have "abused the abilities given to us for no other reason than to follow the clearest evidence and the strongest probability."[1]

For Diderot, believing without the support of clear evidence and strong probability meant that one suffered from a distinctive kind of "weakness of spirit." This is how he defined credulity. For him, credulity is a vice not because of the content of the credulous belief but because of the method of arriving at it. In other words, credulity

A Fake Saint and the True Church. Stefania Tutino, Oxford University Press. © Oxford University Press 2021. DOI: 10.1093/oso/9780197578803.003.0006

is not the sin of believing something false but rather the sin of believing something "without discernment." For Diderot there was a direct link between credulity and falsity: since credulous people have in effect given up on using their reason, "credulity is the vice most suitable to lying."[2]

Diderot was careful not to equate credulity and religion, however, and his fellow encyclopedist André Morellet devoted most of his long entry on the term "faith" to demonstrate that believing in Christian dogmas was not necessarily an act of blind obedience and superstition. For Morellet, professing the Christian faith could be the consequence of a *persuasion raisonnée*, a "reasonable persuasion" based on the "credibility" of specific tenets of Christianity.[3] Other Enlightenment thinkers were much more radical in arguing that credulity and superstition found a fertile ground in religion, and more specifically in Catholicism. For instance, in his *Treatise of Human Nature*, Hume called the Roman Catholic Religion a "strange superstition" whose believers were "fond of the relicts of saints and holy men." He devoted a long section of his *Enquiry Concerning Human Understanding* to a powerful criticism of miracles and other prodigious and supernatural occurrences, which, he thought, people believed out of "superstitious credulity" because they lack "sufficient judgment" to examine "critically" evidence and probability.[4] Voltaire, another harsh critic of credulity, believed that the inability to weigh evidence and probability had terrible effects not only on the ways in which men and women lived their lives, but also on how they reasoned about the past. In his numerous historical and historiographical works, Voltaire ridiculed his predecessors' penchant for fanciful conjectures, unreasonable divine interventions, and dubious evidence. He insisted that true history should be simultaneously critical and philosophical, based on stringent documentary analysis and aimed at revealing and promoting the progress of reason.

The reflections of Diderot, Hume, and Voltaire point to a characteristic that we tend to consider quintessentially modern, differentiating us from our early modern predecessors. In these philosophers' accounts, modernity was born precisely when reason became the criterion to judge a belief worthy of being believed. While pre-modern people tended to hold on to beliefs without discernment, modern people can use their reason to distinguish between solid evidence and improbable conjectures, and consequently to separate reasonable belief from superstitious credulity. The Enlightenment account did not simply provide a historical trajectory from credulity to reasonable belief: It also suggested that such a trajectory was fundamentally irreversible. In this narrative, the progress of reason might happen by fits and starts, and many obstacles and setbacks would occur along the way, but as soon as men and women got a glimpse of the power of human reason, there was no turning back to the cave of ignorance and superstition.

Nowadays we have some evidence that the progress of reason might not be as irreversible as the Enlightenment philosophers anticipated. Even in modern society there are pockets of credulity that remain obstinately resistant to tests of probability and evidence. Several people have expressed anxiety over the future of our civilization, fearing that without the compass of reason, our society will have a hard time navigating the ocean of fake news, rumors, and various manifestations of "truthiness." I am more interested in demonstrating that the Enlightenment account might be equally inaccurate as far as the past was concerned. Investigating the Roman Curia's reception of the fake prophet Giovanni Calà is a good way to illuminate the shortcomings of the traditional narrative.

I don't believe that early modern society was inherently more credulous (in Diderot's sense) than our own society, or that early modern people were incapable of evaluating evidence and weighing probability to distinguish what was reasonably credible from what was utterly incredible. Of course, there are differences between the early modern world and our own. To begin with the most macroscopic difference, early modern people lived in a cultural, intellectual, and social environment in which human truths coexisted with supernatural truths. The presence of the divine was at the center not only of people's daily lives but of their epistemological universe. But the fact that religion occupied a central place in early modern Europe does not mean that all Europeans were unable to use reason to distinguish the fake from the authentic. They were no more congenitally liable than we are to be exploited by anyone who had the means and opportunity to take advantage of their (alleged) mindless credulity.

Naturally, some people were better than others at sorting out the authentic from the fake, just as some people are today. The criteria that early modern people used to distinguish fact from fiction were not much different from our own, but they had a different set of priorities and were confronted by a different set of challenges when it came to the relationship between truth and authenticity. This made the task of deciding what was true and what was false distinctively complex. The case of Carlo Calà and his fake ancestor Giovanni is an excellent window into this complexity.

Catholic theologians knew that it was not possible to fully authenticate the truth of an individual's supernatural charisma by human means. Nevertheless it was possible—indeed necessary— to identify and condemn any fake and fraudulent simulation of sanctity. Catholic theologians also understood that the truth of the facts about a prospective saint's life and deeds was not the same as the truth of Catholic doctrine. When Orazio Quaranta censured Gregorio's biography of Joachim of Fiore, he recognized the difference between authenticating Joachim's status as a true prophet (and the supernatural nature of his friend Giovanni's deeds) and confirming that the book promoting Joachim's ancient cult was consonant with the doctrine of the Church. Quaranta might have wished that he did not have to choose between these two things, but, when faced with the choice, he knew he was responsible only for the latter. But the leaders of the Roman Curia soon realized that it was not easy to separate the truth of history from the truth of theology, and the case of Giovanni Calà both exposed and magnified these difficulties.

As I said at the outset of this chapter, to the eyes of many modern readers, the story of the Calabrian saint must immediately appear too farfetched to be credible. We do not have a monopoly on the hermeneutics of suspicion, however. Very soon after the publication of Carlo Calà's Italian book on Giovanni in 1660, many began to question the authenticity of the story. By the early 1660s, the city of Naples was buzzing with gossip concerning the duke's fake ancestor. Rumors began to spread that the books and manuscripts that Carlo had acquired, allegedly original and ancient, were nothing but forgeries, and that the relics found in 1654 were highly dubious.

Initially, the archbishop of Naples ignored the rumors. The archbishop, as we have seen, had not only provided his assistance in locating the relics and officially recording the sources and documents, but had quickly and generously provided approbation for the duke's Italian treatise on Giovanni. Moreover, given the nature of his position as the local representative of the Church, he was mindful of the need to keep the relationship with the Neapolitan government cordial. Since the Duke of Diano was a powerful representative of the viceregal government, we can understand the archbishop's lack of zeal in verifying rumors that would potentially offend the duke.

However, the archbishop was not the only source of ecclesiastical and theological authority in the city. The Neapolitan *ministro*, or representative, of the Holy Office was also tasked with enforcing the purity and orthodoxy of the Catholic doctrine in Naples. As a Roman agent, the *ministro* of the Inquisition was much freer than his local partner from the web of local patronage and political, social, and economic favors. As soon as he heard the gossip, the Neapolitan *ministro* (Monsignor Alessandro Crescenzi, bishop of Bitonto) began a discreet investigation on behalf of the Roman Inquisition, while his Roman colleagues began a closer examination of the Italian book that the duke had published in 1660.

Crescenzi's task was challenging. Since no evidence of fraud had been discovered, no charges could be brought against the duke. First, Crescenzi had to gather enough information about the possible crime (and the duke's role in it) to initiate an official trial. This initial investigative phase was extremely delicate, and discretion was of the essence. When building their case against a suspect, local Inquisitors needed to identify potential witnesses, persons of interest, or accomplices to the crime, to provide testimonies and relevant evidence to incriminate the suspect. The Inquisitors (or, in some cases, the parish priests who learned of the crime through parishioners' confessions) usually encouraged these witnesses or accomplices to come forward to the tribunal and testify against the main suspect. These individuals were reassured that acting as *sponte comparentes,* that is, reporting to the Inquisition voluntarily as opposed to being coerced to appear at an official trial, would result in a much more lenient punishment than if they were named as codefendants. Once the local Inquisitors had collected as many testimonies and as much evidence as possible against the main suspect, they would transmit all the material to Rome. There, the cardinals of the Holy Office would decide whether to press charges and, if they did so, how to go about making an arrest.

The preliminary investigation had to be conducted with the utmost secrecy, because it was crucial that the main suspects did not hear that a case was being made against them until the moment of arrest. Otherwise they might conceal evidence, intimidate witnesses, or flee the region to avoid capture. In this case, Monsignor Crescenzi certainly realized the importance of discretion. He could not ignore Carlo Calà's prestigious and powerful position, and feared that if the duke got any hint that an Inquisitorial investigation was coming his way, he would use his connections within the viceregal government and archiepiscopal court to avoid prosecution.

Another problem that Crescenzi faced was Ferrante Stocchi, the author of the (allegedly) forged documents. By 1663, he had died.

Therefore the *ministro* could not get hold of the one person who knew for certain not only whether the story of Giovanni was fake, but also whether Carlo Calà had actively instigated the fraud. Calà might simply be the most illustrious of its victims. Moreover, the geography and topography of the world of Catholic censorship was complicated, especially in this case. The affair of the blessed Giovanni covered a rather large territory, from Rome, to Naples, to Calabria and the southern edge of the Neapolitan kingdom. It encompassed not only large cities but small towns and rural areas. The Neapolitan *ministro* had to gather information that was scattered far and wide, at a time when communication between different dioceses was often difficult and slow. And the Duke of Diano could count on many supporters and clients both in Naples and in the Cosenza area, so it was not easy to find witnesses willing or able to cooperate with the investigation.

Finally, the structure of the Roman Inquisition carried its own peculiar difficulties. The Holy Office was a relatively nimble bureaucratic apparatus tightly controlled by the Roman center, but it had to identify and punish a wide variety of doctrinal deviations. Although the Roman Inquisition conducted its activities with a relatively high level of efficiency, things frequently fell through the cracks because of the disparity between the centralization of the tribunals and the scattered nature of crimes, suspects, and evidence. Sometimes local Inquisitors, feeling as if they had been asked to look for a needle in a haystack, gave up searching for information because they thought it would be just too difficult to obtain. At other times, the process of gathering intelligence on a case might yield surprising results. Once an Inquisitor started digging within a local community, who knew what might be found?

Conscious of all these difficulties, Crescenzi dutifully began investigating, and by the beginning of the 1660s, his legwork had started to pay off. On February 15, 1664, the *ministro* finally convinced a cleric by the name of Tommaso Garofalo to testify in the Calà case. Garofalo reported that "three years before," the recently deceased Calabrian forger Stocchi had personally confessed the "scam" to him. Stocchi told Garofalo that "he had delivered to the bishop of Cassano" in the diocese of Cosenza "the bones of some animals," under the pretense that they belonged to Giovanni Calà. In addition to recounting what he had heard from Stocchi, Garofalo testified that another one of his acquaintances, Giuseppe Guerra, also knew of the fraud. Guerra had told him that Stocchi was responsible not only for the fake relics but also for forging the lead ball containing the manuscript biography of Giovanni, as well as the other manuscripts narrating "the glories of the Calà family as well as the life and deeds of the blessed Giovanni." After producing the fake manuscript documents, Guerra told Garofalo that Stocchi had hired a criminal named Giovanni di Luna to "plant" the material "in the Vatican Library."[5]

But Tommaso Garofalo was not the only person of interest identified by the Neapolitan *ministro*. Thanks to a tip provided by the entourage of the archbishop of Naples, Crescenzi had arrived at the name of the Jesuit father Pietro Giustiniani, who was the confessor of one of the perpetrators of the fraud (possibly Stocchi himself?). His knowledge of the forgery was not exactly first-hand, but it was at least reliable, and its authenticity was guaranteed by the obligation of sincerity entailed by the sacrament of confession.

By 1663, Giustiniani was living in the Puglia region in the southern part of the kingdom of Naples—"the heel of the boot" of the Italian peninsula—teaching in one of the local Jesuit schools. From Naples, Monsignor Crescenzi alerted the archbishop of Lecce that the Inquisition wanted to question Giustiniani "in the affair concerning Carlo Calà." Since the Holy Office did not want to wait for Giustiniani to come to Naples, Crescenzi asked the archbishop of Lecce to call him in and conduct the preliminary interrogation locally. The archbishop complied with the orders, and when he started talking with the Jesuit father, he found out much more than he expected.

As was the usual practice in such investigations, Giustiniani was first asked whether he knew the cause of the interrogation. This procedure was followed so that if the suspect professed ignorance, it was possible to accuse him or her of lying. Giustiniani answered that yes, he could "guess why he was being questioned: his teaching on the doctrine of the Eucharist." Asked to elaborate, Giustiniani confessed that the year before, during a discussion with "some of his pupils and other theologians," he had made an unorthodox argument about the Eucharist. He agreed that at the moment of consecration, the bread turned into the body of Christ, but he also believed that Christ might decide to withdraw from the sacrament immediately after the consecration. Consequently nobody should be held to believe, as an article of faith, that Christ's body remained in the bread forever after consecration.

His interlocutors were shocked at Giustiniani's views, and therefore he had composed a small text to distribute to his pupils. In this he explained the rationale for his opinion and demonstrated that it was not necessarily contrary to the doctrine of the Eucharist as promulgated at the Council of Trent. Giustiniani also told the archbishop that "a few months" after composing the text, he realized that his opinion verged dangerously on the heretical. At that point he told his pupils to give back the text he had distributed and issued a short statement in which he declared himself to have made a mistake.[6]

When the archbishop of Lecce learned about this, he was immediately on high alert. Meddling with the doctrine of real presence was very dangerous in the 1660s. In addition to Protestant attacks, the Church had to fend off opposition from Cartesian and atomist philosophers, who challenged the traditional explanation that the sacrament of the Eucharist transformed the substance (i.e., the internal essence) of bread into the substance of the body of Christ, while the accident (i.e., the external appearance) of the bread remained unchanged to the human eye. Atomist philosophers believed that matter was not composed of a combination of substance and accident, but rather of individual atoms: if that was the case, then, how was it possible to explain the changing of the bread into the body of Christ?

Given the urgency of the debate over the Eucharist, the archbishop decided to table the question of the blessed Giovanni and to focus on this new problem instead. Once Monsignor Crescenzi was informed of this unexpected development, he agreed with his Pugliese colleague's decision to prioritize a potentially heretical error over the story of a forged saint. Crescenzi reported the whole matter to Rome, remarking that Giustiniani's mistake was especially worrisome because Giustiniani's voluntary abjuration seemed to him "a bit too curt" to be sincere.[7]

At the end of August 1664, after examining all the relevant material, the cardinals of the Holy Office agreed that Giustiniani's self-abjuration was not sufficient. They sent Lecce the text of a more thorough abjuration for Giustiniani to sign and share with his pupils "on the first day of class" in the fall.[8] On September 10, 1664, the archbishop of Lecce informed the Holy Office that he had "immediately complied" with the orders received; Giustiniani had already signed the abjuration and had been ordered to share it with his pupils on the first day of class when the academic year resumed. Even though the archbishop "had learned that a substitute professor of theology" was coming to teach in Giustiniani's place, he agreed with the rector of the Jesuit college that "it is necessary that Father Giustiniani hold the first class" to deliver his abjuration. The archbishop had also learned that Giustiniani was being transferred "to another college," but once again the archbishop had arranged with the local hierarchy of the Society that Giustiniani "could not leave town unless he obeyed to the orders" of the Holy Office.[9] At the beginning of November, the archbishop informed the Roman Inquisitors that "last Monday, Giustiniani officially abjured his teaching in the first class, in front of all pupils."[10]

After the case concerning Giustiniani's view on the Eucharist was settled, the Neapolitan *ministro* was finally ready to interrogate him about the Calà affair. In the spring of 1665, Crescenzi summoned Giustiniani to Naples, where Giustiniani agreed to testify that Carlo Calà's book "was completely bogus and the relics were fake." Giustiniani told Crescenzi that the source of this information was "an accomplice to the fraud who confessed the crime to him"; he had given Giustiniani "permission to disclose the crime" after his death but without revealing his name. During the confession, Giustiniani learned that the anonymous penitent had forged both the relics and the sources on which Calà's book was based. The penitent also confessed to having hired "a man of ill-repute named Francesco di Luna" to bring the manuscripts to Rome, put them "by fraud" into the collections of the Angelica and Vatican Libraries, and have them registered "by an official notary." Further, the penitent confessed to have forged yet "another manuscript attesting to the sanctity of life of the blessed Giovanni," which he had personally brought to a monastery in Cosenza and gotten officially notarized.[11]

As the *ministro* continued his interrogation, more details emerged. After forging all these documents, the anonymous penitent admitted to Giustiniani that he had gone to the monastery of San Giovanni in Fiore and asked the monks to lend him "a printed book containing the prophecies made by Joachim." The penitent had used some "special water" to "erase the letters from some pages," on which "he later printed a few prophecies concerning the blessed Giovanni." Finally, the penitent told Giustiniani that he had personally written a substantial part of Carlo Calà's book *Historia de' Svevi* and had completely "fabricated the miracles of his own accord."[12]

Giustiniani's testimony was basically consistent with the testimony provided by the other witness Tommaso Garofalo (although they disagreed on whether the criminal responsible for planting the fake sources was named Francesco or Giovanni di Luna). Taken together, the two reports undoubtedly confirmed that the story of Giovanni Calà was entirely fake, and that the main author of the forgery had been Ferrante Stocchi. Crescenzi sent all of the materials he had uncovered to Rome, but he had at least two reasons for disappointment in the results of his investigation. First, neither Giustiniani's nor Garofalo's depositions clarified the Duke of Diano's role in orchestrating the fraud, so Crescenzi still had no evidence of foul play by the duke. The second, and more serious, problem was that both Giustiniani and Garofalo had no direct knowledge of the fraud; their testimonies were based solely on second- or third-hand information, which in a juridical context amounted to nothing but hearsay. Unfortunately, the *ministro* did not think that he could find other means to corroborate their testimonies. Giustiniani's penitent had given him permission to report the content of a confession, and thus to break the confessional seal, only on the condition of anonymity. Besides, the penitent was dead by the time Giustiniani was called to testify, so that road was closed. The criminal Giovanni or Francesco di Luna was nowhere to be found, and even though Crescenzi had come across names of other Calabrian people who might have been involved in the fraud, he "did not think he was going to be able to find other evidence" by interrogating them, "because they are all clients of the Duke or members of his household."[13] The investigation of the Neapolitan *ministro* seemed to have reached a dead end.

Meanwhile the Roman authorities were still examining *Historia de' Svevi,* the book published by Carlo Calà in Italian in 1660. And Calà was working on getting his enlarged version of the book published: the two-volume *De gestis Svevorum,* written in Latin so as to publicize Giovanni's story to a wider audience. By 1663 the book was ready for press, and the duke had already asked the archbishop of Naples to appoint the required reviewers to examine the treatise and eventually to give the final approbation.

Since the archiepiscopal court had officially steered clear of the investigation conducted by the Inquisitorial *ministro,* when Carlo Calà submitted his text for examination, the archbishop had no choice but to follow the regular procedure. Therefore, he passed the book on to two reviewers. The first was Gaetano d'Afflitto, a Theatine father and *consultor* of the Neapolitan Holy Office; the other was Scipione Paolucci, a Jesuit professor of theology in the local Jesuit college. Given the secrecy with which the *ministro* had acted, neither could refrain from the task because of the current investigation, which they either didn't know about, or, if they did, could not in any way disclose. Thus they proceeded to their reviews as normal.

By the beginning of 1664, both reports were in. While d'Afflitto enthusiastically endorsed the book, Paolucci, possibly aware of the suspicions harbored by the Holy Office, expressed some reservations. In his report, Paolucci admitted that Giovanni's miracles and feats of superhuman "strength and courage" as a soldier were "so strange as to produce admiration rather than credence." Nevertheless, he noted that these unbelievable deeds had been confirmed by "a massive number of manuscripts," which "seemed to be authentic" given that they had been written "in very old paper." In addition, there were "letters, coins, epitaphs, and printed works" uncovered by the duke "from libraries and archives," and thus "from the very bosom of antiquity, so to speak." All of those sources had been authenticated "by the testimony of public notaries," and thus couldn't possibly be doubted; rather, they must be treated as the "light of truth." Finally, Paolucci was not tasked with verifying the authenticity of these sources and thus establishing the factual truth of Giovanni's life and deeds; rather, his "only task" was to make sure that the book contained "no offense" against Catholic doctrine and morality. The Latin book was perfectly orthodox in content, and it had all the criteria that Pope Urban VIII had requested for hagiographies of yet-unofficial holy people. Albeit less enthusiastically than his other fellow reviewer, Paolucci also gave his permission.[14]

In 1664 the *ministro* of the Inquisition in Naples was in the middle of his own secret investigation into the story of the blessed Giovanni. As soon as he heard that the archbishop's reviewers had given their approbation to the duke's Latin book, he wrote to inform the Holy Office in Rome. Despite the suspicions and rumors, the duke's book was about to be published with the archbishop's official permission. In the spring of 1664, the cardinals of the Inquisition wrote directly to the archbishop of Naples, ordering him to "get in touch" with the *ministro* and familiarize himself with the most recent developments of his investigation before granting permission to publish Calà's book. The *ministro*, for his part, should share the witnesses' depositions with the archbishop and keep the Congregation "informed" of any new finding.[15]

In the meantime, Carlo Calà had been informed of the favorable reports on his book. With nothing else standing in the way of his masterpiece's publication, he sent the book to press. The duke's *De gestis Svevorum* was published in 1665 by the press of Novello de Bonis, the official printer of the archiepiscopal court. Carlo Calà was so sure of the success of his story that in the spring of 1665 he petitioned the Master of the Sacred Palace, who controlled the printing and distribution of books in Rome, for permission to publish "a second edition" of *De gestis Svevorum* in Rome.[16]

In August of the same year, a very excited Carlo Calà sent a letter to Athanasius Kircher, thanking him for sending a copy of his latest work, *Arithmologia*. The duke alerted Kircher that while researching the genealogy of the Calà family, he had "found out that a lady who married one of my ancestors and whose name was Costanza Conti" was part of Kircher's family lineage. Carlo had found a commemorative medal concerning Kircher's female relative "in a monastery," but there was no need to give any more detail by letter; Carlo "hoped to soon be able to send" to Kircher "the two volumes of *De gestis Svevorum*," in which Kircher could find all the details.[17]

At this point it was no longer possible to ignore the latent conflicts of interest between the Roman Curia, who wanted to expose what appeared more and more likely to be a case of forgery, and the local Neapolitan clergy, who wanted to avoid antagonizing an ambitious fellow citizen. The entire affair was threatening to become a huge source of embarrassment for the Catholic Church. Just as one of the Roman Curia's Inquisitorial officers was conducting a secret investigation for fraud, the main suspect was spreading the fake story wider and wider, aided and abetted by none other than the archbishop of Naples. How could the Curia justify that?

The archbishop of Naples, Cardinal Ascanio Filomarino, was in a difficult spot. He had received clear orders from Rome to stop the publication of Carlo Calà's Latin sequel about the life and deeds of Giovanni, and to help investigate what looked like a fraud. But he had already approved the earlier Italian version of the book years before, and he was reluctant to oppose the Duke of Diano. The duke was only trying to increase the prestige of his household by fostering veneration of a saint, after all, which attested to the duke's Christian zeal. Given the continuous sources of conflict between the Catholic leaders and the Neapolitan administration, the archbishop wanted to avoid spoiling what seemed like a perfect opportunity to foster harmony, not discord, between the upper echelon of the viceregal government and the Neapolitan ecclesiastical leadership. He knew that he had not proceeded with the appropriate caution in this affair, and the only strategy he could think of now was to pass the buck.

The archbishop of Naples admitted to the Roman Inquisitors that the source of all the trouble was his original mistake in allowing Carlo Calà to publish his Italian book in 1660. Nevertheless, he pointed out that "at the time, I did not have the information that I have now"; at that point the rumors of forgery had not yet begun to circulate, and the Inquisitorial *ministro* had not initiated any investigation into the matter. Regardless of what had happened in the past, the archbishop was now fully conscious that the time had come to "get to the clarity of truth." He agreed that it was necessary to find some "remedy" to make up for the damage provoked by the publication of both the Italian and Latin versions of the story of Giovanni.[18]

The archbishop was mindful of the power that Carlo Calà exercised within the viceregal government. He believed that pitting the Neapolitan ecclesiastical leaders directly against the duke would not be advantageous for the Church, because it would render the local ecclesiastical hierarchy even more vulnerable to the attacks of viceregal officers. Therefore, the archbishop thought the best option would be to handle this delicate affair not from Naples, but from Rome.

Accordingly, the archbishop asked the Congregation of the Index to send him a letter in which the cardinals laid out a new policy concerning biographies of yet-unofficial holy people. It was important that the Holy Office write this letter in "general terms," to avoid giving the duke any "opportunity to suspect" that he was the main (and only) target of this new policy. The Roman Inquisitors should state that local bishops and their reviewers were "no longer allowed to issue any approbation" for books containing "miracles, prophecies, and supernatural favors obtained by the intercession of people who are not canonized by the Holy See." If an author wanted to publish such a book, he should "provide evidence" of his sources in the form of "books and manuscripts." The task of verifying the authenticity of the sources was reserved for the Holy See, which alone could give the final approbation.

The problem, however, was that Carlo had already printed his book. To make sure that his elaborate plot did not amount to a case of closing the stable door after the horse has bolted, the archbishop asked the Holy Office to specify an additional requirement. "In the event that perhaps some books have already been published without following the new procedure," the author should still "present to the Roman Inquisitors all the evidence and sources on which the book was based" and wait for the result of their examination.[19]

Finally the archbishop turned to the matter of the allegedly fake relics. They "seem to be all preserved in the area around Castrovillari" in Calabria, and were out of the archbishop's jurisdiction. Since it was not possible for the archbishop and his officers "to gain any kind of information whatsoever" on them, the Holy Office had to find another way to deal with that issue.[20]

The members of the Holy Office must have realized that the archbishop's suggestions were largely motivated by self-interest. Although it was no longer possible for the archbishop to avoid the problem, he did not want to be the one to bear the brunt of Carlo Calà's anger. At the same time, the cardinals of the Inquisition knew that amplifying the clash between the secular and ecclesiastical authorities in Naples would not be beneficial to the Roman Curia, given the history of local conflicts between the viceregal government and the Nepolitan church. Transferring the case from Naples to Rome would ensure a more thorough and impartial analysis of the material, given that the Curia had a number of theologians, ecclesiastical historians, and erudite scholars who could give their opinion without having to worry about political, social, or economic repercussions.

For all of these reasons, after the cardinals of the Roman Inquisition had considered the archbishop's proposal, they saw its benefits and approved it. Since no direct evidence had been found against the duke, no charges could be brought against him. Until the Roman Curia could find a way to investigate and examine the relics in Calabria, the only materials the Roman Inquisitors had to work with were the duke's Italian and Latin books and the allegedly original documents that he had uncovered.

Examining books and manuscripts, however, was the task of the Congregation of the Index of Prohibited Books, not the Inquisition. Therefore, in the summer of 1664, the Holy Office appointed Giacinto Libelli, at that time both the Master of the Sacred Palace and Secretary of the Congregation of the Index, to "write the letter" that the archbishop had requested and send it to Naples.[21] Now the ball was in the court of the Roman Curia.

6

The Roman Curia Takes Over

As soon as the archbishop of Naples received Libelli's letter requesting that all biographies of not-yet-canonized people be vetted in Rome, he passed it on to Carlo Calà. He must have breathed a large sigh of relief that the problem was now out of his hands. The Duke of Diano, on the other hand, was not at all pleased. Not only was the Roman Curia intent on examining his books, but it had also requested that he send to Rome the original documents and sources on which the books were based. As a man accustomed to throwing his weight around, the duke immediately complained about this new—and, from his perspective, unexpected—development by writing directly to Cardinal Marzio Ginetti. Ginetti was a veteran of the Roman censorship apparatus (he had been appointed as a member of the Holy Office in 1629 by Pope Urban VIII), who had been serving as the Prefect of the Congregation of the Index since 1661.

In his letter to Cardinal Ginetti, the Duke of Diano explained that the Neapolitan archbishop, on behalf of the Curia, had ordered him to send to Rome both his printed books and "all the evidence" he had used to support his accounts of the life and deeds of his ancestor. He insisted that such an order was not appropriate. First, his books were "already published," having accommodated the requisite "approbations" and "reviews" commissioned by both the archbishop and the viceroy. The books were effectively a reprint of "several booklets and manuscripts written by ancient clergymen and historians," as well as "other original documents and remarkable testimonies from those times." Moreover, all of those documents had been "officially seen and authenticated several

A Fake Saint and the True Church. Stefania Tutino, Oxford University Press. © Oxford University Press 2021. DOI: 10.1093/oso/9780197578803.003.0007

times" by the public authorities. Finally, the duke's books were fully compliant with papal laws regulating the publishing of books narrating the life and deeds of as-yet-unofficial holy people. For these reasons, a new revision by the Roman Curia seemed both unnecessary and unduly vexing for a loyal member of the Church and prominent member of the Neapolitan government. The duke asked Cardinal Ginetti to either waive the requirement altogether or, if this was not possible, at least to "commission this further examination or report to a Neapolitan authority." There the duke could certainly use his contacts to obtain the outcome he desired.[1]

At the beginning of September 1665, Ginetti notified his colleagues at the Congregation of the Index of the duke's request, but the cardinals did not waver. They had Ginetti write back to the duke reiterating the order to send copies of his books, manuscripts, and printed sources so that they could be properly examined. In the meantime, the members of the Index also decided to relate all the material to "Monsignor assessor of the Holy Office," to keep their Inquisition colleagues in the loop.[2]

By 1666, Carlo had reluctantly agreed to send some of his sources to Rome, where the Congregation of the Index entrusted one of its *revisores*, Stefano Gradi, to proceed with the examination. Stefano Gradi (or, in his native Dalmatian, Gradič) was a remarkable character in the erudite culture of the Roman Curia of his time. He had completed his studies at the Roman College and at the University of Bologna, where he obtained the degree of doctor in civil and canon law, or *in utroque iure*. By the 1650s Gradi had settled in Rome, where he served as a papal diplomat (in 1656 he had been appointed as the official representative in the Holy See for the Republic of Ragusa) and fostered multifarious intellectual interests.

Gradi was especially fond of eloquence and poetry, and had published a collection of his Latin poems in 1660. As a testament to his rhetorical skills, in 1657 Pope Alexander VII chose Gradi as the secretary *ab epistulis Latinis* (a sort of official ghost writer for Latin correspondence) for his cardinal nephew Flavio

Chigi. Pope Alexander VII also appointed Gradi as a *consultor* of the Congregation of the Index and, in 1661, *custos* of the Vatican Library. Upon the death of Alexander VII, Gradi was given the prestigious task of composing the inaugural oration at the conclave that elected Pope Clement IX.

In the following years, Gradi solidified his place as a protagonist in the Roman cultural scene. He cultivated a wide network of erudite correspondents both in Italy and abroad, and assumed an increasingly central role within the *Accademia dei Ricovrati* in Padua and the Academy of Queen Christina of Sweden. Throughout the 1670s, Gradi became acquainted with the new Galilean science. In 1680 he published his *Dissertationes physico-mathematicae*, dedicated to Queen Christina and devoted to physical and astronomical problems such as the nature of accelerated motion. Gradi was also interested in mathematics, and was one of the favorite interlocutors of the distinguished mathematician and Cardinal Michelangelo Ricci. In the dedicatory epistle of his 1666 *Geometrica Exercitatio,* Ricci publicly praised Gradi's "penetrating acumen" in discussing mathematical questions.[3] The crowning achievement of Gradi's career came at the beginning of 1682, with his appointment as the Prefect of the Vatican Library. There he distinguished himself with an aggressive campaign of acquiring both printed and manuscript material.

As soon as Gradi glanced at Carlo Calà's texts, he felt that something was not right. Gradi had perused "with great diligence" several "historical works," including the most recent and authoritative catalogues of saints and martyrs of the Roman Church, but he had not found "even a single mention of the blessed Giovanni Calà" in any of them. Given this glaring absence, Gradi thought that if Carlo wanted to disseminate the story of his ancestor, he would need to provide "evidence" in three distinctive areas.[4] First and foremost, Gradi believed that Carlo would need to "prove" that Giovanni deserved the title of "blessed" according to the official Roman definition of the term. "Simply saying that Giovanni Calà was a man of great virtue and sanctity" and had been able to "perform great miracles" was not going to be good enough. Second, Carlo had to prove that Giovanni was in fact endowed with prophetic spirit. Finally, Carlo had to bring evidence of his ancestor's miracles.[5]

Gradi specified that the manuscripts that Carlo Calà had used and quoted in his text did not qualify as such "evidence." Their authenticity was questionable, and thus "the Apostolic See does not judge them to be a sufficient testimony for such an important question." Giovanni's already dubious story could not be corroborated by equally dubious evidence. Moreover, the locations, authors, and chain of transmission of some of the manuscripts were also obscure and suspicious; in order for the book to be approved, "all authors and manuscripts mentioned need to be known to the Apostolic See and deemed worthy of authority."[6]

When the Duke of Diano heard of Gradi's initial comments, he was indignant. At the beginning of February 1666, he wrote to the secretary of the Congregation of the Index, complaining that the "difficulties" created by Gradi over his books had no merit. As he had already stated, all of the sources had been properly authenticated by the public notaries. More importantly, the Roman Curia had tacitly approved the story of Giovanni well before the duke sought to publish the Latin treatise. Carlo reminded the Roman authorities of "two books," both printed by 1660: one was Gregorio de Laude's biography of Joachim of Fiore, and the other was the duke's very own Italian treatise. Those books, the duke continued, "had been reviewed time and again" in both Naples and Rome. Gregorio's biography in particular had already been "singled out, examined, and approved by the very same Congregation of the Index" that was now raising so many problems. How could the Congregation proceed in what was effectively an attempt to disavow its own previous decision? Once Gradi and his colleagues realized the paradox, they would surely concede that there was no point in denying to Giovanni the "honors that his great charisma deserves."[7]

Undeterred by this pressure, Gradi and his colleagues of the Index continued in their examination. In September of 1666, Gradi was ready to give his full report, or *votum*, to the Congregation. He was merciless. Right from the beginning, Gradi stated that the "lust" (*libido*) to produce forgeries and lies had always infected the history, and thus also the true doctrine, of the Church. The books written by the Duke of Diano provided a "splendid opportunity" to remedy such a dangerous and long-standing disease.[8] It was true, Gradi continued, that the duke's texts contained many parts that were consonant with the doctrine of the Church and that "wonderfully excite the reader to the love of God and to the zeal of devotion." Yet, among all of these "splendid and wonderful virtues," Gradi wrote, "I especially require one, which is by far the most important: truth." Without truth, for Gradi, devotion was meaningless. In this case, "the scope and dimension" of Giovanni's alleged supernatural powers, and consequently the devotion that the powers were supposed to foster, gave Gradi "more and more reason to doubt" the authenticity of the story.[9]

After this preamble, Gradi catalogued his proofs that the book was based on a fraud. He began with a negative argument: How was it possible that until recently no mention had been made of Giovanni, a man of such incredible strength, power, and supernatural charisma? Even assuming that recent ecclesiastical historians such as Cesare Baronio might have ignored Giovanni for some reason (not an easy assumption to make), Giovanni's story was so extravagantly amazing that it was difficult to believe that older, and less historically rigorous, writers might have missed it. How had Giovanni's life not even made an appearance among the medieval hagiographies in *The Golden Legend* by Jacobus de Varagine? This was an author, Gradi remarked, "who has been widely accused of relying on very flimsy reports in this genre of history."[10]

Gradi knew that the goal of all hagiographies, including those based on "flimsy" records, was to promote the veneration for the cult of saints, which was undoubtedly in line with Catholic orthodoxy. Nevertheless, Gradi was aware that fraud and falsity horribly tainted the Catholic faith. Finding a balance between historical authenticity and pious devotion was not an easy task, but as a proud member of the learned community of his time, he believed that the Church could not shy away from it. He remarked that the Church had already faced the dilemma of how to reconcile scholarly rigor and doctrinal orthodoxy several times in the past.

Gradi explicitly mentioned the case of the writings previously attributed to Dionysius the Areopagite (an Athenian judge said to have been converted to Christianity by the Apostle Paul in the first century). These were actually written by an anonymous author in the late fifth or early sixth century, commonly referred to as "pseudo-Dionysius." While the attribution of those works to Dionysius the Areopagite remained largely undisputed in the Middle Ages, several Humanist scholars—most notably Lorenzo Valla and Erasmus—had begun contesting it for a number of philological and historical reasons.

Gradi believed that the pseudo-Dionysian texts "were full of most profound and true doctrine," mostly because they brought relatively strong arguments in favor of the primacy of the pope. Unfortunately, numerous Protestant theologians had used the Humanists' scholarly arguments against Dionysius's authorship as an excuse to attack the papacy. Despite the inconvenience for the Church, Gradi believed it was impossible to ignore their evidence against the attribution, especially because "the catalogues written by St. Jerome and other ancient Fathers made no mention of Dionysius the Areopagite as the author of those works." If absence of corroboration was a strong enough reason to question the authorship of the Dionysian texts, despite their theological and polemical value against the Protestants, how could we give credence to Giovanni's story? It was not only much less plausible and theologically significant, but had "emerged from the grave" very suddenly, after centuries of total and absolute silence.[11]

Leaving aside hagiographies and ecclesiastical histories, Gradi noted that Giovanni and his brother Enrico were supposed to have played an important role within the Holy Roman Empire. How was it possible that no secular historian had recorded anything about them? The duke had attributed the lack of records to the Angevins, who, once they managed to expel the Hohenstaufen dynasty from the kingdom of Sicily, "saw to it that all testimonies of their enemies were destroyed." But how could the Angevins, who did not rule for long, "impose not simply silence, but indeed oblivion" for so many centuries?[12]

Finally, according to Carlo Calà's account, the blessed Giovanni had performed "numerous miracles and prodigies well after his own death." How had the "enemies" of the family managed to prevent the beneficiaries of such frequent graces from being recorded for such a long period of time? The duke's explanation was that it was all part of a divine plan, for "God wanted to postpone the full disclosure of these miracles to glorify the papacy of Alexander VII." Gradi thought that attributing the long silence to the divine providence was basically a cop-out, "like cutting a knot because we are unable to untie it." Highlighting the providential role of Alexander VII's papacy was nothing but an attempt to "flatter the judge with empty praise," when the duke should have tried to "make his case by means of the necessary proofs."[13]

Thus far in his report, Gradi had used only negative arguments, that is, arguments based on the absence of evidence, to challenge the story of Giovanni. As an active protagonist of the erudite circles of his time, Gradi was aware that several other historians, both secular and ecclesiastic, were beginning to "look down on negative arguments" in historical scholarship.[14] A good example of the new critics of the negative argument was the Benedictine scholar Jean Mabillon. Together with his confreres in the Congregation of Saint Maur or Maurists, he had made significant contributions to the development of seventeenth-century textual criticism and historical research. Although Mabillon often used and defended the value of negative arguments, he admitted that a scholar who relies on "purely negative arguments" might be "more easily mistaken" than a scholar who used a negative argument together with a positive one.[15] Thus, Gradi knew that the most effective way to discredit Giovanni's story was not only to point out that no one had ever mentioned it but to present evidence that demonstrated "the absurdity" of it.[16]

Luckily for Gradi, there was no shortage of absurdities in the material he had examined. Starting with the printed sources, Gradi noted that the biography of Giovanni allegedly written by Giovanni's companion Martinus Schener contained not only several improbable events, but also numerous historical mistakes, anachronisms, and errors of chronology. To begin with, Martinus had written that Giovanni was born in 1184. Since "according to all historians," Henry VI's expedition to conquer Southern Italy took place in the spring and summer of 1191, we must conclude that Giovanni was but "a seven-year old boy" when he "fought and won in all those battles."[17] Further, Martinus's biography included an allegedly original letter written by Joachim of Fiore to Henry's wife Constance and dated August 1, 1191. In this letter, the Calabrian prophet alerted the Emperor's wife that Giovanni "had left behind" his military career to become a hermit, and that "by then he was already performing miracles." If this document were authentic, Gradi noted, "then all of the military feats accomplished by Giovanni would have occurred within the space of only three months." How could one young boy "lay siege to Salerno, win against a giant, impress the Emperor to the point of being entrusted with the leadership of Calabria, be mortally wounded, and finally receive the divine medicine that allowed him to regain his health" in such a short period of time? This account was so implausible that "we should rightly suspect that Joachim's letter was fabricated by an impostor, evidently completely ignorant of the events of that time."[18]

The second printed biography, allegedly written by the twelfth-century hermit Johannes Bonatius, did not fare much better.

To Gradi's eyes, it was chock-full of "absurd events, improbable occurrences, and stupid nonsense." One example was its repetition of the legend that Constance had been a nun before marrying Henry VI; this was a sign that the author of the text was either "a collector of vulgar gossip" or "in bad faith."[19] The text contained glaring anachronisms demonstrating that "these writings are meaningless and fake," such as the use of the first-person singular pronoun in the pope's letters (as opposed to the usual first-person plural) or the label of "Father" for Giovanni Calà, who had never been ordained as a priest. Gradi also noted the frequent use of the expression "kingdom of Naples." This usage was "much more recent" than the times in which Bonatius supposedly lived, when the southern part of the Italian peninsula was "commonly referred to as the Duchy of Puglia and Calabria and the Principality of Capua." In the twelfth and thirteenth centuries, "writers could not know" that all these different political entities in southern Italy would be unified under one kingdom and that the city of Naples would be its capital. Instead of assuming that "those writers were able to predict the future," Gradi thought it more probable that the text had been fabricated by "some recent authors who tried to imitate the medieval style but did not know the appropriate terms."[20]

As suspicious as the printed sources were, however, the manuscripts were even worse. They were so obviously fake that the fact that Carlo Calà had submitted them "in such a candid and straightforward manner" made Gradi suspect that he was "very far from having committed the forgery, and in fact he deserves no other reproach than that of being excessively credulous when it came to the glory of his ancestors."[21]

Some of the manuscripts were composed "in a style that is bizarre rather than ancient." The paper on which they were written seemed to have been manipulated with "some kind of dye," which only strengthened Gradi's suspicion that the texts were forged. Other manuscripts were obviously interpolated, and some others were written in what appeared to be a modern hand trying to "imitate" the medieval style. Gradi noted that "the handwriting is never slanted straight or on the right, as is common, but always on the left, which is what usually happens when a writer wants to conceal his own handwriting."[22]

Along with the manuscript material, the Duke of Diano had submitted a number of "patent letters, privileges," and other official documents which Gradi also believed were fake. Some were written on paper, which was itself a certain sign that they were forged. "Nobody in the thirteenth century used paper, or, if they did, they used paper made out of cotton, which is smooth and thick and completely different from the one I have seen in these documents, which appears to be thin and made of out fragments of linen fabric, as we would normally do today." The yellowish color of the paper, moreover, was not the kind that Gradi would have expected to see in aged documents, but seemed rather "artfully created by applying some kind of dirt." Other documents were on parchment, which was more appropriate for medieval documents, but even so they contained no evidence "attesting to their authenticity."[23]

Among the samples Gradi had received was a manuscript account of Giovanni's life and deeds composed by Angelus Primus, a Cistercian monk and supposed companion of Joachim of Fiore. This manuscript had been found in the Angelica library in Rome and had been officially notarized. At this point, Gradi could not know that this was a fake manuscript that had been delivered to Rome by the criminal Giovanni or Francesco di Luna. Nevertheless, the fact that the manuscript had been located in the library and been officially recorded was not sufficient to convince Gradi of its authenticity. The Angelica library was not "that old"; it had been established in 1604, centuries after the manuscript had allegedly been composed. The manuscript's chain of transmission was dubious, as "the custodians say that the manuscript was donated to the library by an unknown person." Finally, the official recording of that document had happened "only a few days" after this mysterious gift. All of these elements, Gradi concluded, contributed to the "strong suspicion that all these actions have been done with fraud and by conspiracy."[24]

In sum, Gradi thought that the duke's Italian and Latin books should not have been allowed to circulate, because they fostered veneration to "a man whose sanctity, and indeed whose very existence, does not appear to be authentic." The "apocryphal testimonies and feigned documents" on which the story was based "strongly suggested" that the story was entirely fake. For these reasons, Gradi felt that "this legend should be cut down at the root." He suggested that the members of the Congregation of the Index "convince the author to send to Rome all of his sources" so that the Index or some other Congregation, such as the Inquisition or the Congregation of Rites, could "issue a definitive judgment" regarding Giovanni's story.[25]

Upon being informed of Gradi's judgment, the Duke of Diano forcefully defended his ancestor. Using his rank in the Neapolitan administration as leverage, he wrote numerous petitions to important members of the Curia to protest what he considered to be unjust and inappropriate treatment of his ancestor. Once again, the duke reminded the Curia that one of the two volumes of *De gestis Svevorum* dealt with Giovanni's life as a soldier; since it touched on no spiritual or ecclesiastical matters, it should be completely outside the jurisdiction of the Index. The second volume, dealing with Giovanni's holiness and prophetic spirit, was based on ancient and officially certified documents, cited already by the duke and by Gregorio de Laude without objections. Carlo Calà found it "incredible that the Holy Congregation of the Index now intends to question what in the past it had solemnly examined and approved."[26]

Seeing that the Congregation was not about to back down, Calà then wrote a long memo responding to the specifics of Gradi's objections. Regarding the fact that no other secular or ecclesiastical historian had ever mentioned Giovanni, there were "infinite cases of saints whose existence had been discovered many centuries after they lived." The much-celebrated new martyrologies and catalogues

of saints such as Baronio's were founded on nothing but newly discovered documents and sources, and "many of those saints had
been included on the basis of only one or two pamphlets." If a few
documents were good enough for saints who had already been
canonized, certainly the case of Giovanni was "all the more impressive, given that by God's favor we have found many hundreds of
testimonies and sources written by ancient saints and clergymen,"
so much so that "simply looking at" such a massive documentary
corpus "inspires veneration and awe."[27]

As any citizen of Naples knew, the politics of sanctity at times
pitted the interests of the Roman Curia against those of its
local flock. Whenever the Curia tried to impose too rigorous a
standard on the cult of a local holy person, the local communities
complained quite vocally. The city of Naples was an especially fertile ground for local unofficial cults. The Catholic authorities were
making efforts to distinguish legitimate devotion from superstition, but they had to tread carefully to avoid an angry reaction
from the mob. Thus, in a polemically adroit and politically astute
move, the duke cast the case of Giovanni in the context of the relationship between the center and the localities of the Church. If
the official Roman catalogues, which listed only "about eighty officially canonized saints," professed to include all of the saints and
blessed of the Church, there would be "very few saints in Paradise."
Thankfully, the heavens were spared such a demographic scarcity
because of the numerous "ancient martyrs and confessors in the
local churches." Despite not being officially included in the Roman
catalogues, they were not "expressly excluded" from the number of
saints either, and in fact their local cult was "officially recognized"
and widely allowed. Why should Giovanni fail to qualify as one
among these "thousands" of local holy people?[28]

On the crucial question of the evidence for Giovanni's sanctity,
Calà made a complete list of the printed and manuscript sources
he had used, clearly demonstrating that the manuscripts were
not only numerous and ancient but also consistent in their story.

Suggesting that such a massive amount of evidence might all be a forgery was tantamount to "denying credence to all the archives and public repositories of churches and monasteries" and "gravely offending all the regal archives, notaries, and registries in which numerous documents pertaining to Giovanni have been stored."[29] All of this material had been fully and officially ratified by public *instrumenta*: "if we were to deny credence to all these inscriptions, certifications, and such like," Calà argued, "we would close the road to the most official and legal proof."[30]

The Duke of Diano composed a second set of responses to Gradi, concerning the chronological errors in the printed sources and the suspicious characteristics of the manuscripts. The duke argued that the alleged authors of some of the works were Giovanni's fellow hermits. They had composed their biographies when they were already old, and it was plausible that they might not remember dates correctly. Even well-respected and celebrated historians occasionally made errors, and such mistakes were "not infrequent in universal chronicles," in which long "digressions" often disturbed the chronological order of the events described.[31] Concerning the question of the manuscripts' antiquity, the duke reminded the erudite censor that ancient paper was known to exist in many different shapes and textures; this should not be surprising, since even modern paper varies dramatically based on the country of its production. Hence, one can find both ancient and current examples of "thick, soft, thin, and all other kinds of paper."[32] Calà claimed that the problems with the ink and the strange colors could be attributed to the tanning process used to "make ancient parchment suitable for writing."[33] On the atypical handwriting, which Gradi deemed a sign of forgery, the duke responded that such doubts were so ridiculous that "the whole city of Rome would laugh at them": "even today there are many people who write in an unusual way and indeed in an odd style."[34]

In sum, in Calà's estimation, none of Gradi's objections seemed worthy of serious consideration. The fact that there were so many manuscripts, and that they had all been fully authenticated by *instrumenta* issued by public authorities, should remove any suspicion of forgery. Calà contended that "only one or two" authoritative manuscripts should be sufficient "not just to obtain permission to publish" but also to allow a public cult and devotion to the blessed Giovanni. The fact that "there are innumerable other manuscripts," all equally authoritative, should serve as "incontrovertible proof" of the sources' authenticity.[35]

Unimpressed with Calà's arrogance, Gradi fought back. The Congregation of the Index was not in the habit of "engaging in discussions with the authors of the books it was supposed to censure." Under normal circumstances, the Index would have completely ignored an author's complaint; in this case, as a token of respect for the status of the duke, "the most that the Congregation can do is to take the objections into account."[36] Coming to the substance of Calà's arguments, for Gradi the whole controversy hinged on the documents' authenticity. The Duke of Diano emphasized that all the manuscripts had been officially authenticated, but Gradi questioned the value of this argument. The Congregation of the Index made its own examination to establish the authenticity of the documents and could not delegate this task to the "will of the notaries." For this reason, the only way to resolve the controversy was for the duke to send all of his material to Rome, where the Congregation could independently inspect and judge its authenticity.[37]

Aside from the question of the authenticity of the sources, there remained the question of the "implausibility" of the narrative. Calà's book contained many improbable and unbelievable things, as well as "numerous and serious errors in matters of history and chronology." Once again, from Gradi's perspective, this required that Calà submit all of his sources to the Congregation. At that point, the Index would appoint "two more reviewers, one of whom should be an expert in antiquities," and in this way could proceed to the full and final examination.[38]

This conflict between Stefano Gradi and Carlo Calà demonstrates a wider debate over the nature and functions of evidence, documents, and archives, and more specifically, over the relationship between legal testimonies and historical sources. Both kinds of documents needed to be authentic in order to be valid, but who was in charge of the process of verification, and which criteria should be used in each case? This question had assumed a particular urgency in the seventeenth century. The process of authenticating legal documents and the process of establishing the authenticity of historical sources had undergone a profound evolution, which in turn changed the ways in which historians, scholars, and jurists thought about the concepts of proof and evidence.

Generally speaking, the early modern notion of legal evidence was based on Roman law, mediated through and supplemented by the interpretations of medieval jurists. By the beginning of the thirteenth century, European jurists agreed that *instrumenta* (official records) were the documents recorded by the public officer titled *tabellio*, or notary. As a public officer, the *tabellio* enjoyed *publica fides*, or public credibility. Therefore all the documents he registered were to be considered *scripturae publicae*, or authoritative official documents. These were different from *scripturae privatae*, "private scriptures," such as informal agreements between private individuals, personal letters, account books, and so on. Because of their status as *scripturae publicae*, the *instrumenta* produced by the *tabellio* enjoyed a series of legal privileges. Most important, public official records were considered as evidence in a court of law; this does not mean they could not be challenged in court, but rather that the challenger had the burden of proving that they were *not* authentic.

As new urban, political, social, and religious institutions emerged and developed, the number and types of archives (places where official documents were stored) multiplied. In late medieval and early modern Europe, archives could be public (such as those kept by the feudal monarchs, and later by the chancelleries of the rulers of city-states and the sovereigns of nation-states), private (established by specific families or associations of merchants and bankers), or ecclesiastical (maintained by local churches, monasteries, religious orders, and, increasingly in early modern times, the centralized authority of the Roman Curia).

With the emergence and consolidation of early modern nation states, there was also an exponential growth of centralized bureaucracies, which used sophisticated large-scale systems of record-keeping. For instance, Philip II king of Spain was a notorious lover of paper: his empire produced a massive amount of records, which the sovereign carefully stored in immense archives such as the one at the castle of Simancas. By the middle of the seventeenth century, the Roman Church had one of the most systematic and wide-reaching networks in early modern Europe for gathering, collecting, and storing information. This information ranged from diplomatic and political correspondence, to Inquisitorial records, to documents pertaining to the global Catholic missionary effort.

As archives grew and multiplied, managing information became more and more crucial for the exercise of power. Archives were not merely passive repositories of documents where knowledge was stored; they became places where knowledge was constantly manipulated and created and where power could find old and new sources of legitimacy. As record-keeping became increasingly central in the political life of Western Europe, archives and document repositories assumed a greater and greater role. Starting in the sixteenth century, European jurists began to reflect more systematically on the nature, birth, and development of archives.

It is easy to see that the nature, role, and functions of notaries as public officers changed to accommodate the novel political, social, and economic needs of late medieval and early modern Europeans. Through all of these changes, however, early modern jurists agreed with their predecessors that the *instrumenta* were endowed with a special authority. This meant that the official recording of a document in an archive conferred to that document a distinctive marker of authenticity. Naturally, early modern jurists realized it was possible for an archival document to be interpolated, incorrect, or outright forged, but they treated this occurrence as an exception rather than a systemic problem. Such an exception should be addressed on a case-by-case basis and resolved by a competent judge in the context of the juridical procedure in which the document was introduced.

As the seventeenth century progressed, however, different political and religious factions within a kingdom began to use archival documents as a means to strengthen their privileges and rights. As legal, juridical, and jurisdictional conflicts multiplied, more and more jurists and intellectuals realized the need for clear and systematic criteria by which to judge the authenticity of archival documents, regardless of provenance.

In the meantime, from the perspective of historical research, the question of how to sort out the authentic from the fake had assumed a crucial role. This was due to the increasingly sophisticated tools for documentary research and philological criticism developed by post-Humanist scholars. As we have seen, ecclesiastical history was not immune to these new developments. Prompted by the need to defend the truth of their respective confessions, both Protestant and Catholic ecclesiastical scholars were often at the forefront of the attempt to erase the stain of forgery from the past. The flip side of this critical attitude in post-Reformation religious conflicts, however, was the emergence of new forms of skepticism. These touched not only on matters of faith but more generally on matters of history and knowledge. The more historians tried to separate facts from fiction, the more discouraged some intellectuals grew about the possibility of finding any certain and reliable evidence of the past. One of these early modern skeptics, François de La Mothe Le Vayer, went so far as to claim that neither history, nor theology, nor any natural science could provide any solid and stable certainty; thus perpetual doubt was the most philosophically correct attitude for a learned person to assume.

In an effort to counter the skeptics, many seventeenth-century ecclesiastical historians (especially those engaged in large-scale research projects, such as the Jesuit Bollandists and the Benedictine Maurists) redoubled their efforts to eliminate forgery from the documented past of the Catholic Church. They also worked to establish more general guidelines for assessing the reliability of historical sources. This would show that, although we might not be able to gain a full and certain knowledge of every historical event, not all historical evidence was doubtful; some facts could be established beyond a reasonable doubt.

This complex scenario had important repercussions for the question of how to establish the authenticity of legal documents. Some intellectuals and ecclesiastical historians believed that jurists and judges needed to apply the same criteria to a legal document that historians applied to historical sources. Jean Mabillon wrote a very influential treatise on this matter, entitled *De re diplomatica*, in 1681. The fact that legal sources were stored in an archive, and thus had been officially entered into the record, did not make the case for their authenticity any stronger. Authenticity depended not on provenance, but on historical and documentary analysis.

Other jurists and intellectuals reacted strongly against this trend. They saw it as a dangerous attempt to undermine not only the special status of the archive as the repository of the *publica fides*, but also the political authority that guaranteed such public faith. Especially in Germany, which was composed of a number of small and fragmented semi-sovereign entities ruled by the Holy Roman emperor, jurists had a considerable role in litigating a myriad of political and jurisdictional cases. Archives (understood as the official repository guaranteed by the political authority) were their most trusted tools. In response to the theories presented by Mabillon and other historians, several late-seventeenth century German jurists opposed any attempt to divest archives of their authority-granting power. They argued that the only valid criterion for authenticating a legal document was the *ius archivii*: the law of the archive. These jurists held that the only repositories of documents deserving the name of archives (as opposed to a mere private collection of papers) were those placed under the sovereignty of the political magistrate; he alone could provide and ensure the *publica fides*. Consequently, as long as a document was proved to have been stored in a legitimate archive, that document had legal value as evidence.

This debate set historians and ecclesiastical scholars on one side and theorists of the *ius archivii* on the other. At stake was the question of the authority needed to establish the authenticity of documents as both historical sources and legally valid testimonies. Could a document be considered authentic just because it was authenticated by the public notary and preserved in a public archive? Or should the assessment of authenticity be based on a critical, philological, and historical examination of the document itself? To deny the former meant undermining the notion of public authority; to deny the latter amounted to sacrificing the tools of critical historical research on the altar of state power.

It is easy to see the profound implications of this seventeenth-century debate for our own society. The identification of two different sets of criteria for authenticating legal testimonies and historical sources is at the core of our modern understanding of the difference between the job of the historian and that of the judge. This difference, in turn, has important consequences for the way in which we think about the process of governing people (through information) and the past (through historical records).

All these elements are clearly visible in Carlo Calà and Stefano Gradi's debate over Carlo's sources regarding the blessed Giovanni. Carlo Calà, on the side of the jurists, believed that the *publica fides* was sufficient to authenticate a document. Even more important, he understood that questioning this principle had the dangerous consequence of "closing the road to the most official and legal proof," jeopardizing the very basis for the legal system of secular government. Carlo thus employed a kind of slippery slope argument. Defending the case of his holy ancestor against Gradi's attacks was not simply a means of safeguarding the nobility and prestige of his own household; it was a way of safeguarding the authority of the legal secular government against the authority of the Church.

Gradi, on the other hand, believed that after documents become historical sources (and not simply legal testimonies), "the will of the notaries" can no longer set the standard for truth. Of course, there is an element of jurisdictional conflict underlying Gradi's position. He was a member of the Curia and thus reluctant to allow Neapolitan notaries to rule over what he believed was properly under the purview of Roman censors. As an erudite scholar, however, Gradi based his attack on the duke's text not on political or jurisdictional considerations but on the need for an accurate critical, and philological scrutiny of documentary sources. In his view, this process should have been completely independent from the process of authentication attested by the *instrumenta*.

The positions of Carlo Calà and Stefano Gradi on the authenticity of these sources were based on two alternative models of looking at the truth of human testimonies. Each had its advantages, and each had its costs. At stake in the case of Giovanni Calà, however, was not only the truth of the past, but also the truth of Catholic doctrine. After all, Giovanni's claim to fame was not only—or even primarily—his (authentic or spurious) deeds. It was his divine gifts and charisma that supposedly rendered those deeds truly supernatural and thus worthy of devotion. As the Roman Curia would soon discover, balancing historical authenticity and religious devotion was not an easy task, and being able to distinguish a forged document from an authentic one was not sufficient to guarantee that the truth would triumph.

7

The Curia at an Impasse

Despite Carlo Calà's valiant efforts, the Roman Curia did not bend
to the "will of the notaries." Wanting to affirm its own jurisdictional and theological authority in authenticating the sources, the
Congregation of the Index endorsed Gradi's judgment and ordered
the Duke of Diano to submit his entire documentary *corpus* to
Rome for examination.

Carlo Calà was enraged. He bombarded the Congregation of
the Index with letters of complaint, stating that he had already sent
many original manuscripts and sources to Rome. He was confident
that "just by looking at them, even the most zealous reviewer would
immediately dispel any doubt concerning their authenticity."
Instead of being satisfied by these voluminous samples, however,
the Congregation now wanted to see all the originals, and Carlo
Calà found this truly unacceptable. The sheer number of sources
was massive; how could the Curia suspect a fraud of such a large
scale? Did the Congregation of the Index really think that "the hundreds of people who wrote those documents" and "the multitude
of public officers and notaries who authenticated them" were all
part of the same conspiracy? Carlo objected that if he were to send
all of his sources to Rome, he might "lose them" or they might be
damaged in the process. He did not want to take that chance. These
documents were "most precious jewels," which he was duty-bound
to preserve "not just for my own sake, but also for the sake of my
successors."[1]

The Curia did not waver, however, and eventually Carlo Calà
caved in. In March of 1669, the Secretary of the Index officially
recorded the arrival of the duke's documents, sent "as evidence of

A Fake Saint and the True Church. Stefania Tutino, Oxford University Press. © Oxford University Press
2021. DOI: 10.1093/oso/9780197578803.003.0008

what he wrote concerning the blessed Giovanni." The Congregation was now ready for the comprehensive examination and final ruling on whether or not to prohibit Carlo's texts.[2]

As was customary for such examinations, the Index appointed three censors to review Carlo's texts. The first, unsurprisingly, was Stefano Gradi, who had been involved with the case since the beginning and had already produced a report in 1666. The other two reviewers were also learned and active participants in the erudite culture of the late seventeenth century. One of them was Ottavio Falconieri, an important figure in the Chigi intellectual entourage and a member of the Academy of Christina of Sweden, the *Accademia del Cimento,* and the *Accademia della Crusca.* It was at the latter that Falconieri had deepened his literary interests. A poet himself, he was instrumental in the scholarly rehabilitation of Torquato Tasso's epic poem *Gerusalemme liberata,* which, despite the vocal criticism of several Italian intellectuals and scholars in those years, went on to become one of the most celebrated works in early modern Italian literature. Like Gradi, Falconieri had eclectic and multifarious intellectual interests. At the end of the 1650s, upon returning from a trip to Northern Europe, he began studying mathematics and astronomy, and became a strong proponent of Galileo's experimental method. In 1666, Pope Alexander VII appointed Falconieri as a *consultor* of the Congregation of the Index, and while in Rome, Falconieri acquired a remarkable competence in antiquities and archaeological finds. At the end of the 1660s he published a few influential works on Roman numismatics and Greek inscriptions.

The third censor was Ludovico Marracci, a Father of the Order of Clerics Regular of the Mother of God, and a leading Arabist in the Curia. Marracci was one of the theologians who oversaw the translation of the Bible into Arabic (eventually printed in 1671), and also authored a widely used Latin translation of the Qur'an. He was a trusted papal adviser and *consultor* of the Index, Inquisition, and *De Propaganda Fide,* and was heavily involved in the conflicts over moral probabilism between Jansenists and Jesuits in the 1660s. While in Rome, Marracci distinguished himself for his moderation in theological debate and his strictness in moral behavior (in 1680, Marracci wrote a pamphlet entitled *Rimedio per curare la vanità femminile* to denounce the immodesty of women's apparel).

Because of these qualities, and because of his widely recognized linguistic abilities, Marracci enjoyed favor in the Curia and was often called upon to establish the authenticity of sources in delicate and difficult cases. For instance, Marracci was a member of the papal committee charged with verifying the authenticity of the so-called *plomos* of Granada, a collection of lead books discovered around Granada at the end of the sixteenth century. These supposedly contained evidence of a pre-Islamic Arabic-speaking Christian community, but were eventually declared to be Muslim forgeries. In 1656, Pope Alexander VII appointed Marracci as the chair of Arabic studies at the University of Rome *La Sapienza*, a post that Marracci occupied for more than forty years until 1699 (he died in February of 1700).

By the fall of 1669, Gradi, Falconieri, and Marracci had completed their reports and submitted them to the Index for discussion. A copy of the full censure by Ottavio Falconieri does not seem to have survived, but it must have been as severe as Gradi's, given that his final judgment on Carlo's books was that they should be "absolutely prohibited."[3] Both Gradi's and Marracci's full final censures are extant, however. The two erudite *consultores* had a high level of scholarly competence and shared the same faith that historical accuracy and documentary authenticity supported, rather than hindered, the truth of the Catholic faith. Nevertheless, the two profoundly disagreed in their judgment of Carlo Calà's texts.

Gradi's 1669 censure was short and sharp. In his 1666 report, Gradi had already indicated that the books did not contain anything against Catholic doctrine, and indeed contained many passages fostering pious devotion to saints. However, the story told in those books was simply not true, for three main reasons. First, all other historians and hagiographers have been "completely silent" on the life and deeds of the blessed Giovanni despite his supposed "great fame" and "memorable accomplishments"; second, the feats ascribed to Giovanni were "improbable and absurd"; and finally, the documents and sources on which the story was based were "made up and fake." The only remaining decision was whether the "falsity of the story contained in this work was worthy of a censure on the part of the Index."[4]

Gradi knew that some people thought (as Orazio Quaranta and Scipione Paolucci certainly did) that the responsibility of the Index did not include deliberating on matters concerning historical truth. Such discussions could be endless and "perhaps it would be impossible to find an author completely trustworthy." Nevertheless, he believed that "since the Christian doctrine contains many things which are either contrary or certainly superior to human reason," it is necessary for the Church to strengthen the belief in authentic miracles, real divine intervention, and legitimate saints. The Church not only can but must engage with historical truth, precisely to distinguish true miracles from shams and protect the "purity and integrity" of its doctrine.[5]

Therefore, given the important issues at stake, and considering that the story of Giovanni was purely fictional, it was legitimate for the Index to prohibit it. The same action had been taken recently for other books concerning saints; like the duke's, these had been printed in compliance with Pope Urban VIII's legislation and contained no heresy or doctrinal error, but were not historically authentic. Gradi reminded his colleagues that in 1659, the Congregation of the Index had examined a collection of letters supposedly written by Giovanni's fellow Calabrian and officially canonized saint Francis of Paola, and collected by Francis's confrere Francesco da Longobardi. The Cardinals of the Index had decided to prohibit that book "not because they found anything contrary to the true doctrine and morality, but because the text contained many things that were absurd, false, and fake."[6]

Committed to the principle that the truth of religion depends on the truth of history, Gradi thought the Index should employ a zero-tolerance policy toward authors who, by failing to respect the latter, sinned against the former. Nevertheless, Gradi was mindful of the rank of the Duke of Diano, and he knew that condemning his books could have severe consequences for the political relationship between the Roman Curia and the kingdom of Naples. The story of Giovanni was certainly a forgery, but prohibiting Carlo Calà's books would send the message that the Roman Curia thought the duke was the forger. In Gradi's opinion, this was not only politically dangerous but untrue. Gradi believed the duke was guilty only of "credulity"; he was the victim of, not a co-conspirator in, a complex and well-orchestrated fraud aimed at appealing to the duke's "naïve" vanity concerning the "deeds of his ancestors."[7] It is worth noting that by 1669, people in Rome had started to talk about Stocchi as the true architect of the forgery. Although the relationship between Stocchi and the duke was not entirely clear (indeed, to this day, it is uncertain what role the duke played in the forgery), Gradi and the rest of the Curia did not wish to examine that aspect of the story too closely.

For all of these reasons, Gradi believed that the case warranted "a special treatment." Instead of prohibiting Carlo's books, it would be best to prohibit only the fake pamphlets and manuscripts on which those texts were based. Given that the duke was not the author of those pamphlets and manuscripts, "his name would not appear in the official decree" of prohibition.[8]

Ludovico Marracci agreed with Gradi on many points. First, like Gradi, Marracci thought that "as far as doctrine and morality are concerned," Carlo's books did not contain "anything worthy of a censure." Indeed, from a doctrinal point of view, Marracci found the duke's texts to be "immensely favorable to the Catholic faith, to the Roman Church, and to the authority and dignity of the Supreme Pontiff, for which the Duke deserved to be praised."[9]

From the standpoint of historical authenticity, Marracci agreed with Gradi that the story of the blessed Giovanni was problematic.

Despite his best efforts, Marracci had not been able to find "even a mention of Giovanni Calà" in the work of "any historian or hagiographer." The entire case for his sanctity, and indeed for his very existence, rested on a large number of manuscript and printed sources. The duke had presented this documentary *corpus* as ancient and original, but many of the sources were "so suspicious" that they carried "little or no authority." In the printed pamphlets, Marracci found several egregious historical and chronological inconsistencies. One was the story, authoritatively disproved by Baronio, that Constance of Hauteville had been a nun prior to her marriage to Henry VI; another was the comment that Roger II had dedicated a hospice to Saint Rocco, who actually lived roughly two centuries later. As Gradi had already done, Marracci noted the glaring anachronisms in the prose, and he also found that the chronology of Giovanni's life did not make sense. How could "a seven-year old boy have been in charge of an imperial army"?[10]

When it came to the manuscripts, Marracci immediately noted that some seemed to have been written in a manner that "imitated" the ancient style but in fact did not seem ancient at all, only "fake and feigned." Like Gradi, Marracci noted that "the type of paper" of these manuscripts was inconsistent with their alleged date, and that the "dyeing substances" appearing on some of the manuscripts "give a strong indication of forgery." Finally, several of the manuscripts had been composed "in the same style even though they were allegedly written by different authors," which again strengthened his suspicion of fraud.[11]

As we can see, Marracci noted exactly the same problems that Gradi had highlighted. What differed, however, was the conclusions that they drew. For Gradi, all of these elements amounted to the certainty that the story of Giovanni was a fraud; for Marracci, the evidence pointed to the fact that Giovanni's story was *probably*, but not certainly, fake. And when it came to matters of saintly devotion and divine interventions, Marracci believed there was a huge difference between probability and certainty.

For Marracci, the chronological errors and anachronisms were not necessarily signs of falsity. They could be excused as "honest historical mistakes," which caused no harm to the doctrinal and theological authority of the Church and were relatively common in historical works that were written long after the events they narrated.[12] Regarding the chronology of Giovanni's life, Marracci admitted it was "difficult" to explain the fact that the printed sources suggested that Giovanni had led the army of the Emperor at the age of seven. Nevertheless, Marracci felt it was possible to defend the authenticity of the pamphlets by arguing, as the Duke of Diano did, that their authors had been old when they composed the texts; a "lapse of memory" might have led them to confuse certain dates.[13]

Regarding the manuscripts, although Marracci found them suspicious at best, he also thought that dating manuscripts was neither easy nor foolproof. A strange-looking style of writing was not always a sign of forgery, because "it can happen that ancient authors use a specific style that over time becomes uncommon." Marracci knew of "several other scholars" who, despite being "most learned," nevertheless "had made mistakes" when they tried to date documents by their style. Marracci reminded his colleagues that "several pious and learned men have already examined" the manuscripts and had "authenticated and officially recorded them as legitimate." Among these men were not only the Neapolitan notaries but also the archbishop of Naples and his reviewers. If the Curia were certain that the manuscripts were fake, then all of these people would be guilty of "either fraud or incompetence." Marracci did not feel ready to make that judgment. Further, although the authenticity of the documents was difficult to prove for certain, establishing with certainty that they had all been forged was even "more difficult and almost impossible." In that case the Curia would have to assume that "several men, including some of high status, had conspired together to forge so many manuscripts and sources and distribute them in so many different places."[14] Finally, Marracci reminded his colleagues that the Congregation of the Index had already "allowed the publication of Gregorio de Laude's biography of Joachim of Fiore," even though that book contained many of the same episodes of Giovanni's life as the duke's work.[15]

In sum, Gradi evidently felt comfortable stating that the evidence demonstrated beyond a reasonable doubt that the blessed Giovanni was a fake. Marracci, on the other hand, was unable to eliminate the ever-so-slight probability that the account held "a kernel of truth."[16] And since the story of Giovanni was, after all, the story of a man touched by divine charisma, Marracci believed the Catholic censors had to be very prudent in using the (probable) evidence of history to evaluate the certain omnipotence of God. Giovanni's life appeared to be characterized by many "prodigious and marvelous" events that defied the laws of physics and the rules of history to the point of "appearing rather incredible." At the same time, however, Marracci reminded the Congregation that legitimate and official saints had been credited with "similar or perhaps even more incredible things"; one should never attempt to circumscribe the power of God within the narrow boundaries of human credibility.[17]

Marracci added that while it was certainly "amazing and incredible" that such a famous, powerful, and holy man as Giovanni had been forgotten for more than four centuries, he also knew that "many famous and important things are often forgotten over time" and emerge only when God's providence deems it appropriate. As an example, Marracci mentioned the case of ancient China. Christianity had once flourished there before being so completely eradicated that no memory of it remained except for the "old stone" unearthed by Jesuit missionaries in the 1620s.[18]

In conclusion, Marracci thought it was "absolutely improbable" that the Duke of Diano was so evil and greedy as to have made up the entire story and forged all the documents to increase the prestige of his already famous and wealthy family. For Marracci, a "more verisimilar" hypothesis was that once upon a time, a man by the name of Giovanni Calà had truly existed. He was indeed pious, but over time people began to exaggerate his holiness and power and to make up fictional miracles. This was known to have happened in the cases of other saints. The duke, for his part, was guilty of nothing but credulity, of which someone might have taken advantage.[19]

For Marracci, this story could not and should not be judged based on a dichotomy between true and false, given that all the arguments for and against its truthfulness were uncertain. Instead, the logic to employ was that of probability: it was probable that Giovanni's story was full of false details, but it was also probable that there was some truth to it. Marracci was well aware that by the middle of the seventeenth century, numerous theologians (especially from the Society of Jesus) had embraced the doctrine of probabilism. They argued that in any situation in which certainty is lacking, all probable courses of action are morally legitimate. The preferable resolution is not necessarily the more probable, but rather the more favorable or least vexing one. One of the probabilists' favorite legal principles was *odia sunt restringenda, favores ampliandi,* or "hateful decisions must be reduced, favorable ones must be increased." Applying probabilist thinking to the case of the blessed Giovanni, Marracci reasoned that the Congregation should take the course of action that proved less damaging "not only to the reputation and honor of the Duke of Diano, but also of those illustrious men who approved his books and provided him with sources."[20] Thus, Marracci concluded, the Index should not prohibit the duke's books. Those works should be allowed to circulate freely, provided that they contained a preface declaring that the permission of the Congregation was not an endorsement of the sanctity of Giovanni and that the cult of Giovanni "was not to be allowed until Giovanni was officially canonized."[21]

When Marracci's colleagues heard his final judgment, they must have been somewhat perplexed. Marracci was effectively allowing the circulation of a story that he himself admitted was for the most part probably fake. In fact, after writing the censure, Marracci felt compelled to add another short text to better explain what he had tried to say in his previous *votum*. He specified that he never meant to judge the truth of Giovanni's sanctity; he simply meant to state that Carlo's books contained nothing against Catholic doctrine. If the cardinals had wanted to know Marracci's opinion on the truth and certainty of the facts, Marracci would have been "at a loss." Following the example of the Athenian judges in the Areopagus, he would have asked for a hundred years before giving his verdict.[22] The entire story of Giovanni was dubious and the evidence shaky; "therefore I would not be able to vouch for his sanctity or his very existence if I were to be asked by judges who inquired not simply about doctrine, but also about the truth of things." Because the Index was the kind of tribunal concerned not with the truth of things but rather with doctrine, the books should be permitted, with the addition of the already mentioned preface.[23]

Returning once again to the question of documentary evidence, Marracci wrote that it was true that some people thought they were forged, but it was also true that others believed in them enough to have officially ratified and authenticated them. For Marracci, this was not a question of legal proof versus historical evidence, but an issue of probability versus certainty. It was improbable that somebody had invented the entire story and falsified all the evidence, just as it was improbable that Giovanni had performed the miraculous and amazing deeds with which he was credited. Finding both sides equally uncertain, Marracci did not feel able to make a definitive judgment one way or the other.

Furthermore, as "difficult" as it was "to pick a side" in this question, that was not the cardinals' task. The Congregation was not asked to decide about the truth of Giovanni Calà's life, but simply to "decide about the doctrinal orthodoxy" of Carlo Calà's devotional texts. Once again, Marracci remarked that the Duke of Diano was an influential man. Prohibiting his books would be not only epistemologically inappropriate but politically inadvisable. The only epistemologically correct, doctrinally legitimate, and politically judicious option would be to allow the books to be printed, while stating explicitly that permission for a book was not the same as endorsement for a saint.[24]

To recapitulate the reasons behind the conflict of opinion between Gradi and Marracci, we should note that Gradi had remained consistent from the beginning. He believed that the truth of history was to be established not by legal and official authentications, but by critical and philological examination. The results of such an examination were crucial to firming up and strengthening the truth of the Catholic faith. Faith was founded on the true divine and supernatural, and thus needed to be thoroughly purified of the stains of human forgery. Marracci agreed with Gradi that the truth of history was always an aid to the truth of doctrine, but he also believed this: while there could never be any doubt concerning the true doctrine, matters of human history included cases in which it was impossible to discern truth from falsity with absolute certainty.

As we have seen, many historians, scholars, and intellectuals in the seventeenth century had noted that in matters of knowledge, uncertainty was often difficult to eliminate completely. Some had taken this attitude to its extreme skeptical conclusion, arguing that a form of perpetual doubt was the most appropriate attitude for learned people to assume toward all aspects of knowledge. Like many of his fellow Catholic scholars, Marracci knew that the tools of criticism and textual analysis were not always conducive to certainty; in fact, the more skilled Catholic scholars became in identifying forgeries, the more doubts and uncertainties they uncovered. Marracci also realized that this growing skepticism was dangerous, because it could lead (and had already led) some intellectuals and scholars to harbor doubts. These doubts concerned not just the reliability of historical knowledge but the certainty of Catholic doctrine—where uncertainty had no place.

Gradi's judgment was based on the inextricable ties between historical truth and theological truth. Marracci argued that unlike the truth of doctrine, which was always absolutely certain, the truth of history was often marred by uncertainty and probability. Thus, if the

Curia wanted to protect both the divinely inspired certainty of the true faith and the integrity of the process of establishing historical authenticity, the only solution was to separate the two. This would ensure that any doubt or uncertainty emerging from the latter did not seep into the former. In the case of the blessed Giovanni, Marracci believed it was impossible to eliminate all traces of doubt; based on all available evidence, the factual truth (or lack thereof) of Giovanni Calà was only probable at best. Consequently, the Curia should not make the mistake of mixing such uncertain truth with the theological (and certain) truth of the Catholic doctrine of saints. For this reason, the duke's books should be allowed because the certainty of their doctrine was sound, regardless of the uncertain truth of their historical content.

If we look at this conflict from the perspective of the relationship between authenticity, credibility, and faith, we can see that it was a symptom of a deeper and more dramatic debate within the Roman Curia. Gradi thought that the truth of Catholic theology could only be saved by embracing the truth of history without fear, and rejecting the false and the fabricated without hesitation. Consequently, he wanted to prohibit texts even if they contained sound doctrine, if such doctrine was based on false facts. Marracci thought that discerning the truth of history was difficult because of the fundamental uncertainty that often characterizes human history. The core task of the Congregation of the Index was to approve the true faith and condemn errors; in order for the system to function, they must keep probability and uncertainty separated from the certainty of Catholic doctrine. Consequently, Marracci recommended approving texts whose factual basis was probably false but whose doctrinal soundness was certain.

Each of these approaches uncovered fundamental and uncomfortable questions. On the one hand, following Gradi's logic, how much can the truth of doctrine depend on the truth of the facts before theology loses its ontological autonomy and becomes simply a branch of ecclesiastical history or philological criticism? On the other hand, using Marracci's reasoning, how much can the truth of doctrine ignore the truth of the facts without being engulfed in the same fiction from which it is supposed to keep its distance?

Behind this debate lies a crucial question involving the very nature of Catholic theology and its relationship to a central feature of modernity: How can the absolute truth of theology relate to, and engage with, the probable certainty of human affairs? How could the supernatural maintain centrality in a world that was increasingly dominated by the human? These questions were already at the center of high-profile conflicts. Examples include the relationship between biblical exegesis, Aristotelianism, and mechanical science during the Galileo affair, and the relationship between philological criticism and theological dogmas in the debate over the authenticity of the Donation of Constantine. The case of the blessed Giovanni Calà demonstrates that these questions were not discussed only in prominent cases involving well-known protagonists; they were seeping into the cracks of what was supposed to be a well-oiled machine whose function was to examine, judge, and sentence.

The story of Carlo and Giovanni Calà might have been a small episode concerning a provincial jurist with great ambitions and a provincial forger with mediocre abilities, but it raised complex and profound questions that the Congregation of the Index was not fully equipped to handle. In fact, after receiving the reports from Falconieri, Gradi, and Marracci, the cardinals were paralyzed.

The three censors' reports were presented at the beginning of September of 1669. Even "after a long discussion," the cardinals could not reach a consensus on how to treat the duke's books. Seizing on Giovanni's status as a prospective saint, they attempted to hand off the hot potato to the Congregation of Rites, the tribunal that adjudicated canonization cases.[25] Pope Clement IX did not like this decision and its implications. The discussion concerned the duke's books, not the veneration of an actual person, and judging books was the responsibility of the Index. He ruled that the cardinals could not delegate a connatural part of their basic duties to the Congregation of Rites; they had to make a decision about the texts. At the end of November 1669, the cardinals went back to the discussion, and found themselves hopelessly deadlocked. Half of them—Marzio Ginetti, Lorenzo Raggi, Francesco Albizzi, and the Neapolitan Ottavio Acquaviva d'Aragona—agreed with Marracci that the books should be allowed if they included a preface declaring that the Congregation did not endorse Giovanni's sanctity and cult. The other half—Carlo Gualterio, Giacomo Filippo Nini, Giacomo Franzoni, and Sigismondo Chigi—insisted on handing the matter over to the Congregation of Rites or to the Inquisition. If this was not possible, Cardinal Sigismondo Chigi thought, the books should be "prohibited altogether."[26]

The records of the Congregation of the Index report the cardinals' different judgments, but we do not have a detailed account of the discussion among the members. We can only conjecture about the motivations behind their disagreement. Sigismondo Chigi, who gave the harshest judgment, was the cardinal nephew of the recently deceased Pope Alexander VII. Sigismondo had been appointed cardinal at the age of eighteen by Alexander VII's successor, Pope Clement IX, just two years before the discussion of the duke's books took place. Presumably Sigismondo was too young and inexperienced to have formed any political alliances in the Congregation that might have influenced his decision to vote for the prohibition; therefore, it is unlikely that his actions were the result of some political or administrative behind-the-scenes agreement. Like his uncle and relatives, Sigismondo was an active protagonist of the cultural life of his time and a collector of manuscripts and books. For this reason, it is more plausible that he was convinced by the erudite arguments put forward by Gradi. Gualterio and Franzoni, on the other hand, were jurists by training; they might have thought that transferring the case to the Inquisition or the Congregation of Rites would be the best way for the Index to avoid any potential problems.

Among the cardinals who supported Marracci's suggestion, it is plausible that Ottavio Acquaviva d'Aragona might have wanted to help out a fellow Neapolitan nobleman. Cardinal Acquaviva was himself a member of the Neapolitan nobility and the nephew of a former archbishop of Naples; he might have been keen to keep the relationship between the Neapolitan aristocracy and the Catholic hierarchy as amicable as possible. Francesco Albizzi, one of the most ardent supporters of Jesuit probabilism in those years, might have been convinced by Marracci's probabilist logic. Ginetti and Raggi, both seasoned members of the papal bureaucratic apparatus, might have thought that following Marracci's suggestion would present the path of least resistance. They might have realized that allowing the duke's books to circulate so long as they contained a disclaimer would serve several goals; it would avoid a potentially dangerous diplomatic crisis with the Neapolitan administration, please the pope (who wanted the Congregation of the Index to make a decision), and protect the Index from responsibility if it turned out that Giovanni Calà was not a saint (or even a real person, for that matter).

Aside from the cardinals' personal background and interests, many other factors could influence how each of them voted in any given case. Papal politics were distinctively mutable and complicated. An appointment to the cardinalate in many ways represented the culmination of an ecclesiastical man's career, because it ensured a relatively stable presence in the Curia, but a cardinal's power inevitably depended on the pope's favor. Thus, every time a new pope was elected, the power dynamics within the Curia changed. Cardinals who wanted to retain their authority had to adjust to the new equilibrium and cultivate the new pope's benevolence. Even though the bureaucratic apparatus of the Catholic Church was relatively solid and efficient by early modern standards, the politics of the Roman Curia were highly susceptible to changes in the power dynamics of the European monarchies; cardinals needed to think wisely about which foreign power they wanted to support. Every issue could represent a potential source of either advancement or trouble, and every opinion a cardinal voiced could gain him the approbation or the disapproval of people who might later become instrumental in advancing his career. As Pope Gregory XV supposedly told his cardinal nephew Ludovico Ludovisi, no pope lasts forever, and therefore Ludovico should plan ahead and move cautiously, "keeping well in mind the future turns of fortune" before taking any action.[27]

For all of these reasons, it is difficult to guess the precise motivations behind the cardinals' votes in the case of the Duke of Diano. What is certain is that the story of the blessed Giovanni was not easy for the Congregation to digest. It is likely that most knew that the sanctity, and indeed the existence, of Giovanni Calà was largely, if not entirely, fictional; on the other hand, they all were aware that the ways in which the Curia reacted to this fictional story could have momentous intellectual, theological, and political implications for the Church.

The members of the Congregation of the Index did not have the opportunity to see the current pope's reaction to their diverging judgment over the case of the blessed Giovanni. A few days after their meeting, in December of 1669, Pope Clement IX died and was succeeded by Clement X. The Duke of Diano had been fully informed of the latest developments and, once again, decided to exert his political influence over the matter before the new pope had a chance to make up his mind. In a petition addressed directly to the newly appointed Pope Clement X, the duke reminded the pontiff that his books had already been examined, reviewed, and discussed several times in the past. Throughout all these years, "everybody had unanimously admitted that the books contained nothing against doctrine and morality." The duke was aware of the results of the latest meeting, in which "half of the Congregation wanted to allow the books with some qualifications, while the other half wanted to pass the case on to the other Congregation." He complained to the pope that it was the Congregation of the Index that had created all of the problems in the first place, given that his books had already been approved by the viceroy and the Neapolitan archbishop. Since the Index had taken the initiative to override the Neapolitan authorities and take the lead in the examination of the books, it should now complete its job and avoid handing over the case to another Congregation, which would have delayed the process unnecessarily and "would have aggravated" the duke "unjustly." From a procedural point of view, the duke concluded, allowing the circulation of his books could not be simpler: Since the members of the Index were split in half, the pope could simply "step in and break the tie." The books could finally be reprinted with the new preface, as Marracci had proposed.[28]

After considering the duke's arguments, Clement X realized that passing the matter over to the Congregation of Rites would be a jurisdictional *faux pas* on the part of the Index. He did not choose to act as tie-breaker and make an executive decision, but at the end of May 1670 he ordered the Congregation of the Index to resume the discussion and "give a definitive sentence."[29] Finally, on June 1, 1670, the cardinals decided to fulfill the duke's wishes: the books would be allowed, provided that they were accompanied by the preface originally suggested by Marracci. Such a preface must be carefully worded, as it needed to navigate a serious ambiguity: How could the Congregation approve a book on Giovanni's holy deeds while simultaneously denying Giovanni's holiness and prohibiting his cult? In view of this difficulty, the pope ordered the cardinals to think this issue over, produce "a draft" of the proposed preface and other related materials, and submit it to the Congregation for yet one more discussion.[30]

The cardinals did what was requested of them and presented their draft in September 1670. Aside from suggesting minor variations to the text, such as deleting a few documents and passages (especially those in which Giovanni Calà was explicitly referred to with the official title of "blessed"), the cardinals required the duke to add a preface. This preface would state that the Congregation of the Index in no way approved any form of devotion to Giovanni, and that the permission to publish the books did not constitute, and should never be used as, an endorsement of Giovanni's sanctity.[31]

When the cardinals met again to examine the text of the proposed preface, however, they once again entered into a "long debate." They would be allowing the circulation of books that described the holy deeds of a man whose sanctity the Congregation did not endorse, whose cult it prohibited, and whose authenticity everybody mistrusted. This would be a bizarre and somewhat contradictory decision, with the potential to put the reputation of the Congregation in serious jeopardy. Thus, in a dramatic turn of events, the cardinals decided to reverse their decision and "prohibit the books altogether."[32]

Carlo Calà did not see this coming. When his informers relayed the decision, he immediately complained to the pope: How could a meeting that was called to discuss a possible preface to his books result in the absolute prohibition of those same books? This sudden turn of events, the duke argued, was evidence that there was "neither rhyme nor reason" behind the prohibition. For Carlo, the cardinals of the Index had no business whatsoever meddling with his books; their task was to monitor doctrine and morality. Since his books contained no fault in either, and indeed "all the reviewers" agreed that they "fostered people's obedience to the Holy Roman Church and pious devotion to God," the Congregation had no grounds on which to prevent his writings from circulating. Finally, the duke resorted to his personal prestige one last time; he reminded the pope that a prohibition was a most serious offense, not only toward the books but toward their author, who did not deserve to be "marred by such a disgraceful stain."[33]

Once again, the pope realized that the duke's arguments had some validity. He must also have thought that satisfying the duke's request was a small price to pay to avoid this steady stream of protests and complaints. Thus, in November 1670, he ordered the Congregation of the Index to resume the discussion. To avoid another deadlock or surprise, this time he committed the matter to somebody close to him, Cardinal Paluzzo Altieri, his cardinal nephew, who, "together with three or four other Cardinals," was charged with revisiting the question and proposing a solution.[34]

The Duke of Diano was on top of this new development, and immediately wrote to Cardinal Altieri to invite him to "proceed to the necessary and appropriate actions" that would allow "his long ordeal" to end with the "right outcome."[35] In November 1671, Cardinal Altieri and his colleagues were ready to recommend to the Congregation of the Index that the books be allowed with the new preface. Once again, however, consensus could not be reached. Five cardinals—Altieri, Francesco Albizzi (who had already voted in favor of the book in 1669), Virginio Orsini, and the Neapolitan cardinals Carlo Carafa and Francesco Maria Brancaccio—favored allowing the books, while all of the others wanted them to be prohibited.[36] At this point, the Congregation gave up. No decision was taken on the matter, and the duke's books remained in a strange limbo: condemned by some members of the Curia, approved (with important qualifications) by others, and acknowledged by all to be doctrinally sound but based on largely false facts.

The failure of the Congregation to come to a decision on Carlo Calà's books is not the only instance in which Rome failed to find a way to link its evolving standards for authenticity, its theological doctrine, and its devotional needs. Over the course of the seventeenth century, the Roman Curia was unable to take a definitive stand on several cases concerning the authenticity of supernatural occurrences, divinely inspired people, and holy relics. Especially after the Council of Trent, the Catholic Church had enforced progressively stricter standards to verify the historical and documentary authenticity of sources, but many unofficial cults to allegedly holy people or objects still existed throughout the Catholic world. Catholic leaders monitored what was happening on the ground, and frequently intervened to shut down cults that turned out to be illegitimate, but often they found that establishing historical or documentary authenticity was in tension with defending the truth of the Catholic faith.

The Catholic Church was institutionally complex. The Roman Curia was in charge of the spiritual well-being and doctrinal orthodoxy of a huge territory, whose geographical horizons were continuously expanding. On paper, the post-Tridentine papacy was supposed to enforce doctrinal and devotional uniformity throughout the Catholic world, but in practice the different local contexts had their own specific religious needs, devotional practices, and cultural habits. As we have seen in Naples, these were not always in step with the will of the Roman center. Finally, the relationship between ecclesiastical and political authorities was often difficult; Naples, again, was a prime example of these difficulties. The Catholic leaders relied on the support of the political sovereigns, but they were fully aware that local political leaders sometimes saw their ecclesiastical counterparts as opponents instead of allies. Not all fights were deemed worth fighting. Sometimes the Catholic hierarchy thought that a conflict with the political leaders was inevitable and necessary; at other times, they decided it was better to let the matter go.

It is not surprising that the Roman Curia was often unable to find the right balance between its historical and documentary standards, the devotional needs of its flock, and the political and economic pressures exercised by local political authorities. This does not mean that Catholic authorities were confused when it came to distinguishing truth from falsity; they were certain that the Catholic religion was true and any opposing or alternative doctrine was not. They were also increasingly more skilled at authenticating sources and identifying historical and documentary forgeries, and they knew that "true" and "authentic" were not always synonyms. What it means, though, is that the relationship between true and authentic was fluid; there was no easy or fixed formula to harmonize historical truth, doctrinal orthodoxy, devotional needs, and political interests. All of these elements existed in a precarious equilibrium that was subject to constant change. Sometimes, as in the case of Carlo and Giovanni Calà, Catholic leaders were unable to find the most appropriate solution. They had no choice but to wait for the right opportunity to present itself before taking any action at all.

8

The End of the Story

In the early 1670s, the Duke of Diano must have been pleased with the developments of the case of his ancestor Giovanni. An approbation would have been ideal, but silence was not a bad outcome either. Carlo decided that the cardinals of the Index had given up on issuing a definitive statement on his books because the Curia was unwilling or unable to put up any significant hurdles to having Giovanni canonized. Taking advantage of the paralysis of the Index, Carlo began to foster the devotion to Giovanni Calà, discreetly but decisively. He began in his native Calabria, where the local clergymen promoted Giovanni's charisma and invited their parishioners to venerate him properly. Once the duke had established Giovanni's cult among his local community, he reasoned, it would be easier to go back to the Curia and ask the Congregation of Rites to begin an official canonization process.

The 1670s began with yet another piece of good news for the duke: the appointment, in 1672, of Antonio Pedro Sancho Dávia y Osorio, Marquis of Astorga, as the new viceroy of Naples. Astorga was a relative of Giovanna Osorio, Carlo's wife, and Carlo did not waste this opportunity to get into the new viceroy's good graces. During Astorga's tenure as the Neapolitan viceroy, Carlo's already remarkable political influence increased. In 1672, Carlo was appointed as *reggente di Cancelleria*, which was the juridical branch of the Collateral Council. Soon after, he became the delegate of the royal jurisdiction, which put him in charge of managing the relationship between ecclesiastical authorities and the viceregal government.

A Fake Saint and the True Church. Stefania Tutino, Oxford University Press. © Oxford University Press 2021. DOI: 10.1093/oso/9780197578803.003.0009

In the early 1670s, Carlo's career was at its peak, and his project of having an official saint join the family seemed within reach. Carlo's crucial position within the viceregal government allowed him to flex his muscles and show his power to the ecclesiastical leaders, while at the same time demonstrating goodwill toward the Church. His skill in this regard is demonstrated by his involvement in a small but significant conflict that pitted the Holy Office against the Neapolitan political leaders at the beginning of the 1670s.

The conflict concerned a particular set of crimes that violated both the secular and the ecclesiastical laws. They were classified by canon law as *mixti fori,* or "of mixed forum." This category included crimes that had both a secular and a spiritual component; for example, bigamy, blasphemy, sorcery, and sacrilegious thefts (thefts of sacred objects and ecclesiastical property). Having more than one wife was against both secular law and the sacrament of matrimony; blasphemy was both a source of scandal that threatened the tranquility of the community and an offense against God. Using magical acts and sorcery to harm people was both a crime against the subjects of the kingdom and an act of defiance against the spiritual authority of God and the Church; stealing, say, a gold or silver pyx in which the Eucharist was stored was a crime against private property and a sacrilegious profanation of the container of the body of Christ.

Because of their dual nature, these crimes could be prosecuted by both the secular and the spiritual court. To avoid potential conflicts between secular and spiritual judges over who should investigate and punish a crime of mixed forum, canon law employed the principle of *praeventio* (from the Latin verb *praevenire,* "to come before" or "to precede"). This stated that whichever judge got to the case first had the right to proceed and sentence the criminal, who could later be sent to the other court if additional punishment was warranted. Heresy was an important exception to the general rule: Since the Holy Office was the only tribunal competent in cases of heresy, if the ecclesiastical or secular judge had reason to believe that heresy had been committed, they had to halt the proceeding immediately and transfer the case to the Inquisition.

Over the course of the sixteenth and especially the seventeenth centuries, the Roman Inquisition invoked the category of heresy more and more frequently in cases of crimes of mixed forum, thus excluding the secular tribunals and retaining for itself the prerogative of judging and punishing the criminals. This was a means of defending and, if possible, enlarging its jurisdiction against the secular tribunals. Secular rulers resisted what they saw as an attempt by the Inquisition to extend its reach in matters that were traditionally under the purview of political magistrates. In a place like Naples, where the tension between the local ecclesiastical leaders, the political government, and the Holy Office was already very high, conflicts concerning the allegedly heretical character of secular or mixed-forum crimes were common. Over the course of the seventeenth century there were a great number of criminals whose prosecution was bitterly contested between the Inquisition and the secular government. Antonio del Piano was one of those criminals.

Antonio was a poor young man, burdened by debt and with a record of petty theft. In the fall of 1672, Antonio set his eyes on some seemingly easy and rewarding loot: the silver pyx used to store the Eucharist in the Church of Saint Francis and Saint Matthew. This was a small and not very popular church in the heart of the poor and rough neighborhood called *Quartieri Spagnoli*, which is today in the historic downtown area of the city. On October 22, Antonio went to the church, waited until he thought he was alone, climbed the stairs to the main altar, forced the tabernacle open, took the silver pyx, hid it under his clothes, and walked away. Unfortunately for Antonio, there had been other people in the church at the time: one priest and one church attendant. The witnesses noticed the young man going up to the altar and leaving the church, and immediately feared the worst. They rushed to the tabernacle, saw that the pyx was missing, and ran after Antonio, chasing him through the alleys around the church while screaming for help. Attracted by the commotion, two women and a man found themselves in Antonio's path and managed to hold him as the government *sbirri*, or policemen, ran to the scene. As Antonio struggled to free himself, the pyx slipped out of his hands and burst open, allowing the consecrated host—the bread which, through the sacrament of the Eucharist, had changed into the body of Christ—to fall onto the ground.

In the meantime, the police arrived on the scene, arrested Antonio, and brought him to the secular tribunal. After a quick interrogation, the judge established that Antonio had tried to steal the silver pyx and thus was guilty of sacrilegious theft, which carried with it the death penalty. At this point, the ecclesiastical authorities got wind of the arrest and moved to convince the secular judge to transfer the case over to the Inquisition. Their grounds were that Antonio had stolen not only the pyx but also the consecrated host within it. For all anybody knew, his target might not have been the silver container but its holy content. Perhaps Antonio planned to use it in some kind of demonic ritual; after all, the consecrated host had ended up on the ground, which might have been deliberate in order to defile the sacrament. Since any attempt to desecrate the body of Christ was a heretical crime, the ecclesiastical authorities believed there was a legitimate suspicion of heresy. This would give the Holy Office alone the right to investigate and punish the crime.

Before the ecclesiastical authorities could make their case to the secular judge, however, the Neapolitan government decided to expedite the death sentence and had Antonio executed by hanging. The viceregal officers decided to make an example out of Antonio's case, to warn people of the swift and merciless treatment awaiting any thief. They cut a hand from Antonio's cadaver and exposed it to the public in the place where the arrest had occurred. Finally, they placed a plaque next to the gruesome relic, to preserve for posterity the cautionary tale of this thief.

When the Neapolitan ecclesiastical authorities learned of this development, they immediately alerted the Holy Office in Rome. The

Roman Inquisitors were enraged; they believed the secular judge knew perfectly well that Antonio's theft involved the sacred host, which, as a consequence of Antonio's action, had been disgracefully "scattered on the ground." Not only was this "a notorious fact throughout the city," but "even the witnesses called to testify against Antonio had confirmed it."[1] Since the judge had been informed of the potentially heretical offense against the consecrated host, he would also have known that the Holy Office alone was competent to judge the crime. Thus, the Roman Inquisitors believed that the Neapolitan government had deliberately ignored the jurisdictional rights of the Church and proceeded to a quick execution to avoid turning the criminal over to the Inquisitorial tribunal.

The Inquisitors were also infuriated by the plaque the government put up at the scene of the crime, which they believed added insult to injury. First, it would serve as a perpetual reminder of the usurpation of authority on the part of the viceroy; second, from the Church's point of view, at the time of his death Antonio had not yet been proven to be a heretic. According to the rules of the Holy Office, the reputation of a suspect had to be protected until he was proven guilty. The plaque installed by the viceregal government would have brought posthumous *infamia*, or infamy, to Antonio's name, which constituted yet another offense against the juridical and jurisdictional authority of the Roman Inquisition.

Given the seriousness of these acts, the Holy Office immediately issued an official complaint to the viceroy and asked him to make amends for the actions of his government. Since Antonio was already dead, the only compensation the Inquisitors could demand was that the commemorative plaque be immediately removed. The viceregal government decided not to comply with the request. They requested Carlo Calà to write an official memo to be presented to the Holy Office, demonstrating that the secular magistrates had done nothing but act according to their right and duty.

In September of 1673, the duke completed his memo and submitted it to the Roman Inquisition. Although the aim of the document was to defend the legitimacy of the viceregal government's actions, the duke's tone was far from confrontational. He made the case that what the government had done was not only legally and jurisdictionally correct but religiously praiseworthy, because it was done with the intention of "manifesting the Viceroy's devotion and reverence toward sacred objects, as well as his most deferential respect toward the authority of the Pope."[2]

Carlo explained that the severity of the sentence and the speed of the execution were not a sign that the secular judges were trying to dodge ecclesiastical justice or denigrate the jurisdiction of the Inquisition. Rather, these actions demonstrated the viceroy's "most ardent desire to avenge a most grave sacrilege" done against the Church. Antonio was punished so swiftly and severely not simply because he had stolen a silver object, but because the silver object in question was the container of the "most sacred host."[3]

Coming to the objections of the Holy Office concerning the suspicion of heresy, Carlo Calà admitted that the secular judges considered the disgrace to the consecrated host to be an aggravating circumstance; this was why Antonio had been declared guilty of sacrilegious, rather than simple, theft. Nevertheless, Carlo firmly denied that the secular judges had willfully ignored the possibly heretical components of the crime. Although Antonio already had a criminal record for petty theft, "he was never suspected or investigated for sortilege of any kind." Further, all of the witnesses at the scene had testified that Antonio did not throw the consecrated host onto the ground purposely. The host had fallen out of the pyx as it slipped from Antonio's grip. Indeed, after the consecrated bread fell onto the ground, Antonio "did not step on it or defile it in any way," which was further evidence that it was "verisimilar that the fall of the host was an accident," and not an indication of Antonio's "intention of committing some kind of heretical sortilege."[4]

The duke remarked that historical precedent was on his side. In the past, the Church had often been more than happy to allow the secular judges to investigate and punish cases involving the theft of sacred objects, so long as there was no evidence that heresy was involved. When there was a legitimate reason to suspect heresy, the officers of the Neapolitan kingdom had been very proactive in giving up their jurisdiction in favor of the Inquisition. Carlo mentioned several recent examples of suspected heretics who had been apprehended by the secular justice and immediately given over to the Inquisition; their trials were still ongoing, several months or even years after the secular authorities had first gotten their hands on them. The duke mentioned this fact "not in order to accuse the ecclesiastical judges of being slow or negligent," but only to reassure the Holy Office that whenever there was a hint of heresy in a crime, everybody in the Neapolitan justice system recognized the right of the Inquisition "with the utmost promptness." The only reason this had not happened in Antonio's case was that there was no reasonable ground to suspect heresy, given that "the criminal had never given any indication, either in words or in deeds," of any heretical intention.[5]

Coming to the question of the plaque, the duke once again defended the government's decision. It was an act of reverence, not of defiance, toward the Holy See. Given that Antonio was guilty of sacrilegious theft and not of heresy, the government had every right to put up the plaque—not to bring infamy to a suspected heretic (which Antonio was not), but "to scare off the people by reminding them of the punishment" for such a grave offense. The fact that the viceregal government took such a crime so seriously should have pleased the Church, because it would have instilled "even more devotion toward the Holy Sacrament" among the Neapolitan people.[6]

Despite the duke's relatively conciliatory tone, the cardinals of the Holy Office did not buy his arguments. They asked the jurist Pietro Serista, who served as the *Procurator fiscalis* of the Roman tribunal (the officer of the Inquisition in charge of formally laying charges against the accused, almost as a prosecutor would do today), to draw up a detailed document in response to the duke's memo. The aim was to demonstrate that the viceregal government had acted in bad faith and overstepped its jurisdictional boundaries.[7] The Inquisitors discussed the duke's report and Serista's answer in the winter of 1673. At the beginning of January 1674, they unanimously agreed that Antonio's theft was a matter pertaining to the Holy Office; therefore the viceregal government needed to make amends by removing the plaque. If the viceroy failed to do so, the pope would excommunicate everyone involved in the affair, from the judge who first interrogated and condemned Antonio, to all of the high officials who had approved the placement of the plaque. In the meantime, the Holy Office ordered the nuncio in Madrid to present a formal complaint to the king of Spain, thus pressuring the Spanish sovereign to intervene with his Neapolitan lieutenant on behalf of Rome.[8]

The Duke of Diano remained convinced that his moderate strategy would pay off. He was sure that the viceroy would be pleased with his work, because his memo effectively made no concession to Rome, and justified both the secular court's jurisdictional right to judge and punish Antonio and the government's decision to erect the plaque. He also believed that the Roman Curia would appreciate his explanation that the government had not intended to oppose the right of the Church, but rather to show respect and devotion toward the Holy See. Carlo was so sure that his rhetorical posture would please the Roman Curia that in the middle of the crisis, in February 1674, he petitioned the Holy Office for the license to read prohibited books. The cardinals of the Holy Office might have appreciated Carlo's moderation, but they were not ready to bury the hatchet quite yet. When they received the duke's petition, they decided to "wait before granting the license requested," and let Carlo stew for a bit until the affair of the plaque was resolved.[9]

All through the winter and spring of 1674, the conflict between the viceregal government and the Holy Office remained at a standstill. Despite protests and threats from Rome and lobbying efforts by the nuncio in Madrid, the viceroy had no intention of backing down; the plaque remained where it was. At the end of

May, the Holy Office decided that the time had come to proceed with the excommunication of all the officers involved. At that point, the viceroy finally recognized that this battle was no longer worth fighting, and he waved the white flag. Later that summer, the *ministro* of the Holy Office in Naples was pleased to inform his Roman colleagues that "on July 21, at 7 pm," the plaque had been removed and substituted with another one. The new plaque did not mention Antonio's name, and gave no details on the theft and punishment; it simply stated that it had been installed by the viceroy to remind the Neapolitan people how serious "crimes against religion" were. The Holy Office, evidently happy with the outcome, ordered the nuncio and the *ministro* to "praise" the viceroy for the wise decision.[10] After the removal of the contested plaque, the Holy Office maintained its side of the bargain and absolved all of the government officials who had been excommunicated. By the beginning of the fall, everybody had received the absolution, and on November 7, the Holy Office granted to Carlo Calà the license to read prohibited books.[11]

Despite its relatively positive resolution, however, this affair led the Roman Curia to realize that Antonio's case and its subsequent developments were not an isolated incident. Immediately after the removal of the plaque, a committee was formed to sketch a policy for dealing with similar cases. Over the following months, the members of the Holy Office discussed the question, and in 1676, Pope Innocent XI officially declared that any theft of a pyx containing the consecrated host was exclusively under the jurisdiction of the Holy Office.[12]

Although this new papal pronouncement was bound to create more friction with the Neapolitan authorities down the line, for the moment Carlo Calà was too busy basking in his success to worry. Not only had he weathered a potentially dangerous storm—he had emerged from the conflict in an even better position than before. It is true that the viceroy had to backtrack regarding the plaque, but the reason for surrendering was not because the duke had failed to defend the government's case strongly enough. It was because the pope had made good on his threat of excommunication, an act that no secular leader or government officer could counter. As far as his own relationship with the Curia was concerned, the duke had reason to believe that the Roman authorities were not particularly angry at him—after all, in the end, the Roman Inquisition had granted him the license to read prohibited books as requested. Finally, in the mid-1670s, the duke had yet another reason to be pleased: The cult to Giovanni was growing steadily in Calabria. Soon the duke would be able to put the final touches on his campaign to have his ancestor canonized.

In the fall of 1678, Carlo decided that the right time had come. He asked Monsignor Giacinto Miceli, the apostolic vicar of the diocese of Cassano (where Castrovillari, Giovanni's birthplace, was located) to issue a decree certifying that the cult of the blessed Giovanni was *ab immemorabili* (i.e., from time immemorial, hence legitimate and authentic). This was the preliminary step toward an official canonization. The duke did not know it yet, but something wicked was coming his way.

Even though the cardinals of the Index had not come to a definitive decision on the duke's books back in the early 1670s, everybody in the Curia was well aware that Giovanni's sanctity was most probably fake. Throughout the 1670s, the Neapolitan *ministro* had continued to keep an eye on the affair of the blessed Giovanni and had kept his Roman colleagues informed of any notable development. At the beginning of February 1678, the *ministro* (Domenico Cennini, bishop of Gravina) had something very interesting to tell his Roman colleagues: Carlo Calà was stepping up his campaign to foster the people's devotion to his ancestor in Calabria by inviting the people to venerate Giovanni's relics, together with a supposedly holy and miraculous image. The Roman Inquisition, headed by Pope Innocent XI, ordered Cennini to keep investigating "secretly" into the matter, to find out whether the supposedly holy image contained a caption that explicitly defined Giovanni as "blessed" and whether Giovanni was depicted "with a halo over his head or with light rays emanating from him."[13]

Unfortunately, the *ministro* was unable to get his hands on the allegedly miraculous image. In the course of his investigation, however, he learned of the decree that Monsignor Miceli had issued to authenticate the cult of the blessed Giovanni. He obtained a copy and sent it to Rome. When the Roman Inquisition received the document, it immediately realized that this new development might turn the tables on the duke. No longer was Giovanni simply the (possibly fake) protagonist of a devotional and edifying story. Monsignor Miceli's decree publicly and formally declared that Giovanni was a *bona fide* holy man and consequently the object of a certified cult—all of which happened with no official vetting or permission by the Curia. In the spring of 1679, the Holy Office decided to dig up all of the documents from the Index concerning the affair from the 1660s onward. It ordered one of its *consultores*, the eminent theologian and future Cardinal Lorenzo Brancati di Lauria, to conduct an "extrajudicial evaluation" of the case. This meant an examination outside of the regular legal proceedings of the Inquisition, prior to setting up an official trial.[14]

While Lauria proceeded with his examination in Rome, back in Naples the *ministro* was experiencing some difficulties. He was supposed to give his Roman colleagues more details on Giovanni's cult and his allegedly miraculous image, but all of the witnesses he tried to interrogate refused to testify, "because they are close to, and financially dependent on, the Duke of Diano."[15] The Roman Inquisitors were aware that finding more evidence in Calabria or Naples would probably be impossible, but they also realized that in the long chain of friends, clients, and helpers of the duke, there was a weak link: Monsignor Miceli, the author of the decree.

Miceli was neither a wealthy man nor a governmental officer, but simply a middling provincial clergyman. Therefore he had the most to lose if he were the target of an Inquisitorial trial, with no safety net to break his fall. At the end of January 1680, Miceli was ordered to come to Rome "as soon as possible," and was officially put on trial at the beginning of the summer.[16] As the Holy Office examined Miceli, all of the previously discussed doubts and concerns regarding the feigned documents, the fake relics, and the falsity of Giovanni's story resurfaced. This time, however, the matter did not concern a book or the question of historical truth and its relationship with doctrine. It concerned actual devotion to a man whose very existence was in question and—most importantly from the Inquisition's point of view—whose saintly status had never been approved by the Curia. The cardinals of the Holy Office had no doubts or hesitations. They proceeded to shut down Giovanni's case once and for all.

On June 5, 1680, the Roman Inquisitors officially declared that Miceli had taken the initiative to authenticate Giovanni's cult without the permission of the Curia. Consequently, they found him guilty of having produced "an invalid and illegitimate act," and postponed any decision on his punishment until the pope ruled on the entire case.[17] On June 27, the pope gave his final and definitive sentence: the bones and relics of the alleged blessed Giovanni were "to be extracted from the burial place" or removed from their sites and "buried in a mass grave"; the images in which Giovanni was portrayed with the attributes of a saint were to be removed; all of the books narrating Giovanni's supposed holy deeds, including those written by the duke, were to be "prohibited"; and all of the manuscripts the duke had used as sources were to be "confiscated and held in the Holy Office among its other records." Miceli was suspended from all his functions and ordered to remain in Rome as a prisoner until the Congregation ruled otherwise. Finally, the Holy Office wanted all the people who had collaborated to spread the cult of the false saint to be admonished for their errors, and it reserved the right to subject them to further trials and penalties.[18]

In August 1680, the *ministro* of the Inquisition in Naples informed the Holy Office that the sentence had been carried out, and copies of it were affixed in all public places in Naples and in

Calabria. This action was "much applauded," but it also provoked "not a small grief to the Duke of Diano, considering his vanity." The Inquisition was pleased with the *ministro's* job and wanted the matter to be communicated to the nuncio in Naples as well, to use as leverage in his own dealings with the Neapolitan administration.[19]

Monsignor Giacinto Miceli recovered pretty quickly from the pope's sentence. Everybody in the Curia knew he was the lowest man on the totem pole in this story, so the Holy Office saw no reason to deny a measure of mercy. In the fall of 1680, the cardinals of the Inquisition allowed him to leave Rome to "go back to his hometown." In January of 1681, they agreed to "rehabilitate him" fully, granting him permission to return to his functions as apostolic vicar.[20] For Carlo Calà, on the other hand, the sentence was a fatal blow. It extinguished all hopes he had for adding a saint to the list of his ancestors, and put an immediate and definitive halt to all the plans and strategies that he had spent more than twenty years concocting. After the pope's sentence, his role in promoting Giovanni, which the duke had hoped would increase his stature, became instead a serious liability. It could not have come at a worse time for his career.

Neapolitan politics was a notoriously difficult and dangerous sport. Because all the political, economic, and social activities of the kingdom centered on the viceregal court, the favor of a viceroy could quickly make or break any career. This was even more true in the case of administrators like Carlo Calà, who emerged from the ranks of the non-noble elite and could not count on the privileges and security afforded by an aristocratic title. Since the beginning of his ascent through the ranks of the Neapolitan bureaucracy, Carlo had been able to use the dynamics of viceregal patronage to his advantage. The appointment of the Viceroy Astorga, Carlo's relative, had seemed like the icing on a cake that Carlo had spent decades baking. But Astorga's tenure, like that of most viceroys in early modern Naples, was short. In 1675, Fernando Fajardo Marquis of Los Vélez replaced Astorga as the new viceroy of Naples.

Everybody at court knew that Carlo was one of the most loyal members of the entourage of the old viceroy. Therefore, as the new leadership settled in, Carlo found himself more and more marginalized. By the end of the 1670s, his political influence had declined considerably, and in 1678 he was forced to give up his post as delegate of the royal jurisdiction.[21] The 1680 sentence of the Inquisition further undercut his declining public profile, and by the early 1680s, the Duke of Diano was no longer one of the movers and shakers in the viceregal government. Instead, he cut a rather pathetic figure; he was still fabulously wealthy but had become politically irrelevant. To many people at court, he was even the subject of scorn and ridicule.

Among the most humiliating moments of this part of the duke's life was an incident that occurred in 1683. It involved the renowned painter Luca Giordano, a favorite of the viceroy Gaspar Méndez de Haro Marquis of Carpio and a very popular painter in Naples, where he had been commissioned to produce numerous works, both big and small. Giordano was in charge of painting the frescoes of the vault of a chapel in the Jesuit Church of the *Gesù Nuovo*. This was supposed to be dedicated to the memory of Carlo's uncle Francesco Merlino, a former regent of the Council of Italy and president of the Sacred Royal Council.

As Giordano's eighteenth-century biographer Bernardo de' Dominici tells the story, despite Giordano's amazing speed and productivity (his ability to have his atelier complete a great volume of paintings in a relatively short time had gained the painter the nickname "Luca *fa presto*," or "work-fast Luca"), he was running late with his work on the Merlino chapel. The viceroy had "kept Giordano busy" with the viceroy's personal commissions. The Duke of Diano was irritated by the delay in completing the chapel that commemorated his dead, famous, and unquestionably real uncle. One day at the end of 1683, when the painter came to give the duke his best wishes for the upcoming new year, the duke reprimanded him for "slacking off" on such an important job.

Upset by the exchange, Giordano told the viceroy about it. The viceroy reassured the painter that the opinion of the Duke of Diano was not worth "worrying about," and that Giordano should give no further thought to the matter. Evidently irritated by the duke's scolding of his favorite painter, the viceroy was not ready to leave it at that, and decided to teach the duke a lesson that would dissuade him once and for all from meddling with Giordano's schedule.

A few days later, the Duke of Diano paid his own courtesy visit to the viceroy for the new year. The viceroy showed Carlo a painting done "in the style of Rubens" without telling him that its painter was Luca Giordano. The viceroy asked the duke to guess the painter. The duke, "who boasted of being able to identify all painters' style," responded that the painting must have been done "by the hand of a bizarre painter in the Flemish school, possibly in Rubens's atelier," and perhaps "even by Rubens himself." Without missing a beat, the viceroy told the duke that he had thought of asking Luca Giordano to do a painting to go along with the one he had just showed him. The duke responded "with a smirk" and proceeded to trash Giordano "at great length," complaining how slow he was. At that point, the viceroy "could not contain himself any longer and bursted out that the painting he just showed to the duke was done by Giordano himself." After this revelation, the viceroy explained that Giordano was so talented that the viceroy thought that the painter was actually "sent by God on earth in order to show just how amazing the most noble art of painting could be." The reason that Giordano was late in completing the Merlino chapel was that the viceroy had "wanted Giordano to finish other paintings" first. Thus, if the duke ever wanted to complain again about the delay on the chapel, he should take this up with "the Viceroy himself, not Luca."[22]

According to Dominici, the duke was so disturbed by this incident that for a few days the only topic on his mind was how "to excuse himself with Luca" and avoid giving him reason to delay his work on the chapel even further, while at the same time remedying his *faux pas* with the viceroy. Unfortunately, before the duke could plan a successful strategy to accomplish these goals, "he came down with an acute fever," from which he never recovered.[23] On December 22, 1683, Carlo died, with neither a saint in his family tree to welcome him in heaven nor an heir to carry on his family legacy on earth. The only thing that Carlo left behind was his wealth, which amounted to the extraordinary sum of 500,000 *ducati*. This was the object of a long and contested legal battle among the duke's distant relatives.

Luca Giordano finished the work on the vault of the Merlino chapel in 1687, but by then Carlo was already dead. He never got the opportunity to "see the completion of the fresco that he so ardently desired."[24] As it turned out, few others were able to see Giordano's finished fresco either, because the vault of the Merlino chapel collapsed during the earthquake of 1688. This not only destroyed Giordano's work but erased what was supposed to be an everlasting tribute to Carlo's real ancestor Francesco Merlino. Today, the chapel is known as the Chapel of the Visitation, because it contains an altarpiece by Massimo Stanzione depicting the visitation of Mary. Aside from Stanzione's work, the only reason the chapel is popular among tourists and devotees is that it holds the relics of Saint Giuseppe Moscati, a medical doctor and public health expert who died in 1927 and was canonized by Pope John Paul II in 1987. As for Carlo's fictitious ancestor, after the duke's death, Giovanni's cult vanished as suddenly as it had appeared, and the story of his amazing charisma sank back into historical oblivion.

The one loose end of this story that cannot be tied up concerns the controversial prophet (and Giovanni's alleged companion) Joachim of Fiore. As the Roman Inquisitors reviewed the relevant material for their final examination and sentence over Giovanni's case, Gregorio de Laude's biography of Joachim came back to their attention. Gregorio's book discussed Giovanni's miracles at length and reported many of the same sources that the duke had used for his account of Giovanni's life. In addition to being tied to a set of newly prohibited texts, Gregorio's book had itself been prohibited "*donec corrigatur*" by the Congregation of the Index in 1662; even though the Index had approved the printing of an emended edition in 1664, no corrected version had ever been produced. Finally, Gregorio's book was problematic because it had been written with the clear aim of promoting Joachim's sanctity. Although Joachim's existence, unlike Giovanni's, was undoubted, his prophetic power and holy miracles remained controversial. For all of these reasons, the Roman Inquisitors wanted to keep an eye on the affair. They ordered the Neapolitan *ministro* to have local ecclesiastical leaders monitor the status of Joachim's cult throughout Southern Italy, and especially in Calabria. Soon enough, the archbishop of Cosenza reported to his superiors that Joachim was indeed the object of a suspicious veneration, especially among the Cistercian monks living in the monastery of San Giovanni in Fiore. Rumor had it that the monks of that monastery called Joachim "blessed" even though the Curia had not yet officially declared him as such. Moreover, they were said to "keep a perpetually lit lamp on an altar built above Joachim's grave," which the archbishop suspected was part of an attempt to "increase the people's veneration" toward Joachim. This rumor was all the more worrisome, the archbishop added, because "these lands are inhabited by a mob of more than 4,000 peasants, the majority of whom are so gullible that they are ready to believe anything." Thus they were eminently susceptible to the monks' attempts to illegitimately "validate" the sanctity of Joachim.[25]

When the Roman Inquisitors heard the news, they ordered the archbishop to investigate the matter further to discover whether the monks were willingly and publicly venerating Joachim as a saint, in defiance of the Holy See. In the fall and winter of 1680, the archbishop of Cosenza, with the assistance of the staff of the Neapolitan tribunal of the Holy Office, officially interrogated several monks who were living or had recently lived in the monastery. They all confirmed that the body of Joachim was below the altar, inside a coffin decorated with his effigy.

Nevertheless, the monks testified that the altar had not been built to encourage people's devotion to Joachim. As one of the monks explained, "in the old days" before the altar had been built, "people used to visit Joachim's tomb and scratch the effigy on his coffin with iron tools, in order to shave off pieces of it." Those pieces were considered to be miraculous relics, which people "used whenever they fell ill."[26] Thus, the monks had decided to cover up the tomb and build the altar to prevent people from damaging the coffin and engaging in such unregulated and superstitious practices.

As for the lit lamp, the monks all told the same version of the story: The initiative to put a lit lamp over the altar had not come from the abbot or even from the monks. Rather, the monks testified that one Antonio Russo, a lay brother whose job was to manage the food supplies of the monastery, had decided of his own accord to light a lamp on Joachim's altar. As soon as the Abbot noticed the lamp, he took it down and "reprimanded" Antonio for having put it there.[27]

By January of 1681, the archbishop of Cosenza had finished interrogating the witnesses, but he had not been able to verify whether the monks' version of the story was true or whether they were all conspiring to cover up an illegitimate attempt to venerate the sanctity of Joachim. The archbishop thought the best course of action would be to send everything over to the Roman Inquisitors and let them decide what to do. In the meantime, the *ministro* in Naples had discovered that a copy of Gregorio's biography of Joachim had been found in the Cosenza area. The *ministro* sent the book to Rome, adding that in his opinion, it was "credible" that Gregorio's book was circulating not only in Calabria, but "also in many other places." In March of 1681, the Cardinals of Holy Office met to discuss all these new developments coming from Cosenza and Naples. In the end they decided to take no direct action, but rather to pass everything on to the Congregation of Rites, to which they entrusted a final decision over the status of Joachim.[28]

To this day the canonization case of Joachim has not come to a conclusion. Joachim's devotees are still waiting for a decision.

Conclusion

As I said at the outset, to conclude my course on the Roman Inquisition I always ask my students what they have learned. Since I do not have the opportunity to do the same for the readers, the best I can do at the end of this book is to state what I hope I have been able to convey. First and foremost, the case of Carlo Calà and his fake ancestor is the story of a forged genealogy. In this respect, it is just one of the innumerable examples of the efforts on the part of the pre-modern elites to find (or, more frequently, create) a noble and holy pedigree, which resulted in a proliferation of fanciful, far-fetched, and often entirely fictitious genealogies. It might be tempting (and, from the point of view of our own modern condition, even comforting) to ascribe the production of all these incredible genealogies to pre-modern credulity, imagining that early modern Europe was populated by people who had no appreciation for the truth of history and no idea what historical research and documentary evidence were. Therefore, we might conclude that our early modern predecessors had neither the cultural and intellectual means to distinguish the fake from the true, nor the philosophical attitude and moral integrity to understand the importance of such a distinction.

Nevertheless, as proud as we might be of our enlightened reason and modern critical attitude toward the truth of the past, we should not forget that a number of historical facts should caution against viewing early modern Catholicism as the apex of groundless credulity. First of all, we should remember that early modern historians and antiquarians shared some important ideological and methodological principles with their modern successors. Indeed, the cornerstones of what we call the modern historical method were first identified and articulated in early modern times. In parallel, the deep and in some cases traumatic political and religious divisions that lacerated early modern European society contributed to put the concern for authenticity into sharper focus. When early modern intellectuals, jurists, and theologians were confronted with a massive number of authoritative texts contradicting one another, they had to step up their efforts to separate the true from the fake, so as to make sure that whatever political or theological side for which they fought was supported by genuine authority.

The need to distinguish truth from falsity, aided by a growing ability to do so, was even more pressing when it came to stories of supernatural charisma and the truth of religion. Early modern Catholic leaders were tasked with defending the absolute truth of their faith against attacks both from their Protestant enemies, and from the growing number of skeptics challenging the truth of any supernatural manifestation. Hence, many Catholic theologians, scholars, and historians—perfectly aware of just how high the stakes were—were especially interested themselves in making sure that the wheat of the true faith did not end up getting mixed with the chaff of falsity, error, and deceit.

All this, of course, does not mean that instances of forgeries and stories of false saints did not abound in the early modern Catholic world. To the contrary, people faked quite a lot of historical facts and documents attesting to the truth of allegedly divine charisma and supernatural interventions. The reasons why early modern people created or relied on fake documents were several. Some forgeries were produced and disseminated for personal gain; others proliferated because they served as tools to assert one's ideological, political, or theological allegiance; still others circulated simply because nobody was able to demonstrate their lack of authenticity. As we saw in the case of Giovanni Calà, all the scholars and theologians involved in examining the sources immediately recognized them as, at best, suspicious, and some of these scholars were absolutely certain that they were the product of forgery. Nevertheless, a combination of theological demands, political opportunism, liturgical needs, and social and cultural pressures prevented the forgery from being exposed as such and allowed it to circulate for years before the Inquisition shut it down.

To be sure, we have better tools at our disposal today than did early modern people, and this is also thanks, in part, to these early modern forgers themselves, given that their very effort to produce forgeries has been pivotal in sharpening their successors' ability to expose them. A further difference separating us from our early modern ancestors is that we have developed a relatively robust commitment to intellectual, not just political, democracy, which allows us to resist any attempt to justify producing or disseminating falsity in the name of a higher truth. Nevertheless, we have not managed to eliminate forgeries completely. Indeed, in many ways the task of distinguishing the real from the fake has gotten more complex, not less, because public platforms for sharing information have multiplied and, in parallel, the traditional modes of sifting, sorting, and evaluating information have been discredited without being replaced by equally authoritative institutions or people in charge of spelling out the criteria for believing or disbelieving. In sum, our society might have become more skilled at authenticating and verifying facts, less willing to consider supernatural truths as the regulating compass of our values and behavior, and more sensitive to the importance of a free exchange of information for a healthy democracy, but the relationship between truth and authenticity is still a challenge for us, as it was for our early modern predecessors.

I believe that recognizing what has changed between the early modern world and our own is as important as recognizing what hasn't, because otherwise we won't understand either the past or each other. When it comes to the dangers we incur if we judge without understanding, the best example I can think of comes from the historian Roberto Bizzocchi. In his book on the significance of fictitious genealogies in early modern European political and cultural life, Bizzocchi related the story of the farmer Kreszentia Deutinger, who lived all her life in a village in Bavaria and died there in 1983, at the age of 85. Everybody in her small community knew that after her death, she wanted to leave her patrimony to her neighbors, but by the time Kreszentia passed away, she still hadn't managed to write a notarized will. Thus, a town clerk who knew the situation decided to forge her will, so that Kreszentia's wish could come true. Once the authorities discovered the forgery, they put the clerk on trial. The evidence they acquired confirmed both that the will was not authentic and that Kreszentia's intention to leave everything to her fellow townspeople had been genuine. Everybody in the village, aware of Kreszentia's desire and of the results of the investigation, was rooting for the clerk, but the judges assigned to the case had to follow the law. In the end, while the judges openly acknowledged that the clerk had produced the document in good faith and with the sole intention of documenting what was in fact Kreszentia's true and authentic wish, nevertheless they also condemned him to serve a sentence of two and a half years in prison for having forged the will.

Ever since I read Bizzocchi's book (which is about twenty-five years ago now), the story of Kreszentia and the forger-clerk has been haunting me, because I have a hard time coming up with a correct judgment over it. Was the clerk right in faking a legal document for the sake of the truth? Were the judges right in punishing the forgery even though forging a will was the only way to make sure that Kreszentia's authentic and legitimate wish would be fulfilled? Is it possible for the outcome of the case to feel wrong even though everybody involved in it did what they felt was right? I certainly do not claim that learning the story of Carlo Calà and his fake ancestor Giovanni has helped me to decide who was right and who was wrong in Kreszentia's case, but it definitely has helped me to see that the relationship between truth and authenticity is not simple, and that sometimes the best (and only) thing I can do is try to understand the complexity involved.

In addition to telling the story of a man and his fake ancestor as a way to showcase the specific complexities of the relationship between truth and authenticity in the context of early modern Catholic culture, this book also tells the story, or at least some parts of it, of a rather large cast of supporting characters, all trying to survive as best they could, each facing his or her own specific challenges.

Once again, the early modern people I have been writing about lived in a very different context from our own, but as we learn to understand these differences, we also learn to appreciate that some things do not change after all. So as unlikely as it is that anybody today would see their career fall apart because they promoted the sanctity of a fake ancestor, we all have seen, and perhaps even experienced, the bitter disappointment of scorned ambition. As unlikely as it is that any geologist today would attribute a volcanic eruption to God's wrath, I believe that all scientists can sympathize with the fear and panic that people feel when confronted with a natural disaster of immense proportions. It is unlikely that any scholarly collaboration today would entail exchanging information concerning the bones of giants and trading favors with the Queen's confessor, but whenever my colleagues and I interact with one another, we are certainly mindful of the delicate equilibrium between academic patronage and scholarly conversation. I don't expect to read in the newspaper anytime soon the story of somebody who was put to death for stealing a sacred object from a church, and yet I do often read of criminals punished with the death penalty and wonder if the punishment truly fits the crime, and whether the sentence was issued in order to send some kind of political message. Finally, it is unlikely that two expert witnesses testifying in a trial would face the same challenges that Stefano Gradi and Ludovico Marracci faced when they were asked to give their judgment over the authenticity of the sources concerning Giovanni Calà, but all of us have felt at one point or another the pain of not knowing how to balance what we think is true with what we think is right.

In sum, I hope that after reading this book, readers will have enjoyed learning things they didn't know about early modern Catholic culture and about life in the seventeenth century. I also hope that in this process, they will have become more sensitive to differences, better equipped at identifying what changes and what doesn't, and more interested in finding out why.

List of Abbreviations

AAV	Archivio Apostolico Vaticano, Vatican City
ACDF	Archivio della Congregazione per la Dottrina della Fede, Vatican City
APUG	Archivio della Pontificia Università Gregoriana, Rome
ARSI	Archivum Romanum Societatis Iesu, Rome
BAV	Biblioteca Apostolica Vaticana, Vatican City
DBI	*Dizionario Biografico degli Italiani*, Rome 1960–

Notes

Chapter 1

1. Francesco D'Andrea, *Ricordi,* ed. by Nino Cortese in *I Ricordi di un Avvocato Napoletano del Seicento* (Naples: Lubrano e C, 1923), 139.
2. Larcando Laco [*vere* Carlo Calà], *Risposta al manifesto del Christianissimo Re di Francia* (Naples, 1648), 63–71.
3. Ibid., 76.
4. *De contrabannis clericorum in rebus extrahi prohibitis a Regno Neapolitano Dissertatio iuridico-politica D.Caroli Calà I.C. in supremis Regni tribunalibus advocati,* s.l. s.d. [*vere* Naples, 1646] .
5. Ibid., 6.
6. Ibid., 13.
7. Ibid., 18–19.
8. Ibid., 106–115.
9. Ibid., 44–46.
10. Ibid., 116–117.
11. ACDF, Index, Diarii IV, 175v–176r. The censures against Vico's book can be found in ACDF, Index, Protocolli GG, 223r–248v.
12. ACDF, Index, Protocolli HH, 301v. Cf. *De contrabannis,* 128.
13. ACDF, Index, Diarii V, 10r–v.
14. D'Andrea, *Ricordi,* 139.
15. Ibid.
16. Ibid.
17. Quot. in Guy Bechtel and Jean-Claude Carrière, *Dictionnaire de la bêtise et des erreurs de jugement* (Paris: Laffont, 1965), 216.
18. BAV, Borg. Lat. 49, 56r.
19. Ibid., 61v–62r.

Chapter 2

1. The story of Stocchi's conversation with Giovanni Maria circulated rather widely in the nineteenth century, and was reported in Louis Gabriel

Michaud's *Biographie universelle ancienne et moderne* (Paris, 1811–1828), s.v. "Stocchi, Ferdinand."

2. The account of the miraculous discovery of the bones and lead ball comes from Paolo Antonio Paoli OMD, a scholar and antiquarian (nephew of Sebastiano, a Catholic erudite clergyman from the same order of the Clerics Regular of the Mother of God who collaborated with Ludovico Antonio Muratori), in *Notizie spettanti all'opera apocrifa intitolata "Storia degli Svevi"* (Rome, 1792), section XV.

3. Among the numerous manuscripts that appeared in the 1650s, at least two are still extant, and they both mention Giovanni Calà in connection with Joachim of Fiore. One of them, BAV Rossiani 480, 1r–5v, is entitled "Prophetiae & Epistolae Ioachini Abbatis Florensis pertinentes ad res Kalabras." It contains eight of Joachim of Fiore's letters and eight of his prophecies. In the letters Joachim mentions Giovanni Calà as a "miles & affinis" (5r, epis.V). The other manuscript, BAV Ferraioli 728, 371r–372v, contains a list of prophecies by both Joachim and Giovanni, and is part of a work allegedly composed by Johannes Bonatius (author of one of the printed pamphlets and of other manuscripts), entitled "De prophetis sui temporis."

4. Carlo Calà, *Historia de' Svevi* (Naples, 1660), dedicatory epistle to the readers, unfol.

5. Ibid.

Chapter 3

1. AAV, Segreteria di Stato, Napoli, 61G, 24r.
2. Ibid., 196v.
3. Ibid., 201r–v.
4. Ibid., 223r–v.
5. Ibid., 220r–221v.
6. ACDF, SO Decreta 1660, 188v.
7. AAV, Segreteria di Stato, Napoli, 61G, 233r–v.
8. Ibid., 234r–v.
9. Ibid., 293v.
10. Ibid., 285r.
11. Ibid., 278r–v.
12. Ibid., 351v.
13. ARSI, FG 663, 306r–v.
14. Kircher, *Diatribe de prodigiosis crucibus* (Rome, 1661).

15. Carlo Calà, *Memorie storiche* (Naples, 1661), 165.

16. Ibid., 184–185.

17. AAV, Segreteria di Stato, Napoli 61 G, 521v.

18. Calà to Kircher, Naples, February 12, 1666, APUG 563, 86r.

19. Calà to Kircher, Naples, July 22, 1663, APUG 555, 193r.

20. Calà to Kircher, Naples, June 22, 1666, APUG 563, 90r.

21. Calà to Kircher, Naples, November 15, 1661, APUG 555, 263r.

22. Calà to Kircher, Naples, December 23, 1661, Ibid., 203v.

23. Kircher, *Mundus Subterraneus* (Amsterdam, 1665), 2 vols., vol. II, Book VIII, Sec. II, Chap. IV, 53.

24. Ibid., 58.

25. Ibid., 62.

26. Calà to Kircher, Naples, May 14, 1666, APUG 563, 279r.

27. Calà to Kircher, Naples, June 22, 1666, Ibid., 90r–v.

Chapter 4

1. Baronio, *Annales Ecclesiastici*, vol. XII (Rome, 1607), 821–822. See also Baronio's manuscript version of this passage, BAV, Vat. Lat. 5694B, 416r–v.

2. *Acta Sanctorum*, vol. VII (Antwerp, 1688), 89–143.

3. Giacomo Greco, *Ioacchim Abbatis et Florensis Ordinis Chronologia* (Cosenza, 1612), 3–4.

4. Ferdinando Ughelli, *Italia Sacra*, vol. IX (Rome, 1662), 262.

5. Ibid., 254.

6. Gregorio's manuscript annals, entitled "Cathalogus Abbatum Sagittariensis Monasterii," can be found in BAV, Barb. Lat. 3247.

7. Gregorio de Laude, *Magni Divinique Prophetae B. Jo. Joachim . . . Hergasiarum Alethia Apologetica, sive Mirabilium Veritas Defensa* (Naples, 1660) , 300.

8. Ibid., 75.

9. Ibid., "Vaticinorum magni Prophetae B. Joannis Joachim de Romanis Pontificibus historica & symbolica explicatio," 13 and 19. The *Vaticinia de summis Pontificibus* was a collection of thirty prophecies, each including a figure, concerning successive popes starting with Nicholas III. The *Vaticinia* were not actually written by Joachim; the first fifteen were written at the beginning of the fourteenth century, probably in a Franciscan Spiritual context. The remaining fifteen started to appear, joined with the previous ones, in manuscripts dating to the late fourteenth century.

10. Ibid., "Obiectionis solutio" and "Auctoris Protestatio," sig. b-verso and b2-recto.
11. Ibid., ch. XLIV, 138–151 at 138.
12. Ibid., ch. LVIII, 256–262 at 257.
13. Ibid., 139.
14. In Gregorio's book there is a marginal note on 139, probably added right before going to press, alerting the readers that Carlo's book had just received the official imprimatur from the archbishop of Naples.
15. ACDF, Index, Protocolli KK, 725r–v.
16. ACDF, Index, Diarii VI, 8 March 1661, 98v.
17. ACDF, Index, Protocolli LL, 102r.
18. Ibid., 102v.
19. Ibid., 102v–103r.
20. Ibid., 118r–121r at 119r.
21. Ibid., 121r.
22. ACDF, Index, Diarii VI, December 19, 1662, 114v.
23. Ibid., January 15, 1664, 128v.
24. ACDF, Index, Protocolli LL, 130r–v.
25. ACDF, Index, Diarii VI, 132r, February 13, 1664, 132r. The date of Gregorio's death is uncertain, but this interaction with the Congregation of the Index seems to be the last record we have of him.
26. *Acta Sanctorum,* vol. VII, 89.

Chapter 5

1. See Denis Diderot's entry *"croire,"* in *Encyclopédie*, vol. 4 (Paris, 1754), 502.
2. Ibid. See Diderot's entry *"crédulité,"* 451–452.
3. See André Morellet's entry *"foi,"* in *Encyclopédie*, vol. 7 (Paris, 1757), 7–23 at 9–11.
4. David Hume, *A Treatise of Human Nature,* (London, 1739–1740), Book I, Part III, Section VIII, and *An Enquiry Concerning Human Understanding,* (London, 1748) Section X.
5. ACDF, St St B 4 h, folder n.18, 108r–v.
6. ACDF, St St O 1 d, folder n.15, 268r–v. See 271r–v for Giustiniani's own explanation of his opinion and his subsequent retraction.
7. Ibid., 268v.
8. Ibid., 273v. The text of the abjuration composed by the Inquisition and sent to the archbishop can be found in 278r–279r.
9. Ibid., 277r–v.
10. Ibid., 282r–v.

11. ACDF, St St B 4 h, folder n.18, 108v–109r.
12. Ibid., 109r–v. A summary of the investigation can also be found in ACDF, St St RR 2 a, 171r–173v (but the pagination in the volume is not consistent).
13. Ibid., 109v (marginal note).
14. Censure of Scipione Paolucci, January 8, 1664, in *De gestis Svevorum*, Naples, 1665, tom.I, unfol.
15. ACDF, SO Decreta 1664, March 4, 38v, and April 2, 52v.
16. ACDF, SO Decreta 1665, 100r.
17. Calà to Kircher, Naples August 15, 1665, APUG 563, 96r.
18. ACDF, Index, Protocolli PP, 306r–307r at 306r.
19. Ibid., 306r–v.
20. Ibid., 307r.
21. ACDF, SO Decreta 1664, July 23, 117v.

Chapter 6

1. ACDF, Index, Protocolli PP, 256r–v.
2. ACDF, Index, Diarii VII, September 1, 1665, 5r–v.
3. Michelangelo Ricci, *Geometrica Exercitatio* (Rome, 1666), dedicatory epistle to Stefano Gradi, unfol.
4. ACDF, Index, Protocolli PP, 286r.
5. Ibid.
6. Ibid., 286r–v. Incidentally, at the Vatican Library there is a copy of the *Historia de' Svevi* coming from the "*Fondo S.Offizio*" (Stamp. S.Offizio 5) in which an anonymous reader (possibly Gradi himself) underlined several parts of the book, especially the introduction in which the duke spoke about the ancient cult of the blessed Giovanni and reproduced the approbations by Cardinal Filomarino and his *revisores* (unfol.), the parts in which the duke narrated the relationship between Giovanni and Joachim of Fiore (see, e.g., 121 and 139), and the sections on the relics and the documentary sources on which Giovanni's story was based (see, e.g., 116, 132, 143, and 170).
7. ACDF, Index, Protocolli PP, 2845–285r.
8. Ibid., fos. 320r–327r, at 320r.
9. Ibid., 321v.
10. Ibid., 321v–322r.
11. Ibid., 322r.
12. Ibid.

13. Ibid., 322v.
14. Ibid.
15. Jean Mabillon, *Traité des études monastiques*, Paris, 1691, 296.
16. ACDF, Index, Protocolli PP, f.322v.
17. Ibid.
18. Ibid., 323r–v.
19. Ibid., 324r–v.
20. Ibid., 324v–325r.
21. Ibid., 325r.
22. Ibid., 325v.
23. Ibid.
24. Ibid., 325r.
25. Ibid., 325v.
26. Ibid., 244r–245r.
27. Ibid., 246r–255v at 247r.
28. Ibid., 247v–248r.
29. Ibid., 253v–254r.
30. Ibid., 254r.
31. Ibid., 234r–239v at 237v.
32. Ibid., 236r.
33. Ibid., 235r.
34. Ibid., 235v–236r.
35. Ibid., 234v–235v.
36. Ibid. 329r–v, at 329r.
37. Ibid.
38. Ibid., 329r–v.

Chapter 7

1. The Duke of Diano to Card. Ginetti, ACDF, Index, Protocolli PP, 240r–243r, at 242r.
2. ACDF, Index, Diarii VII, March 27, 1669, 23v.
3. ACDF, Index, Protocolli QQ, 177r–178r at 177r.
4. ACDF, Index, Protocolli PP, 332r–333v at 332r.
5. Ibid., 332r–332v.
6. Ibid., 332v–333r.
7. Ibid., 333r.
8. Ibid.
9. Ibid., 312r–315v at 312r–v.

10. Ibid., 312r–314v.

11. Ibid., 313v–314r.

12. Ibid., 312r and 314r–v.

13. Ibid., 314r–v.

14. Ibid.

15. Ibid., 315v.

16. Ibid.

17. Ibid., 314v.

18. Ibid., 314v–315r. Marracci is referring here to the so-called Nestorian Monument, a stele found by the Jesuits in 1625 near modern-day Xi'an and containing a bilingual Chinese-Syriac inscription, which for the Jesuits was a testament to the presence of Nestorian communities in 7th-century Northern China. Its authenticity was defended by Athanasius Kircher in his *China Illustrata* and denied by many seventeenth- and eighteenth-century intellectuals, including Voltaire.

19. ACDF, Index, Protocolli PP, 315r–v.

20. Ibid.

21. Ibid.

22. Ibid., 316r–v at 316r. The episode Marracci referred to was narrated by Ammianus Marcellinus (*Rerum Gestarum Libri* 29.2.19). It concerned a woman from Smyrna who confessed to Dolabella (Roman proconsul of Asia) to have poisoned her husband and son because she learned that they had killed another of her sons from a previous marriage. Uncertain about the sentence, Dolabella referred the matter to the Areopagus (the highest tribunal in Athens). The judges told the woman to return to them for the sentence in a hundred years: given the gravity and difficulty of the matter, they did not want to decide hastily and risk acquitting a murderer or condemning somebody who rightly avenged a crime. As Ammianus put it, "something for which there is no turning back is never considered late" (*numquam tardum existimatur, quod est omnium ultimum*).

23. ACDF, Index, Protocolli PP, 316r.

24. Ibid., 316r–v.

25. ACDF, Index, Diarii VII, September 3, 1669, 25v–26r, and ACDF, Index, Protocolli PP, 310r.

26. ACDF, Index, Diarii VII, November 26, 1669, 27r.

27. Quot. in Mario Rosa, *La Curia Romana nell'ETÀ moderna*, Rome: Viella, 2013, 175.

28. ACDF, Index, Protocolli PP, 300r.

29. ACDF, Index, Diarii VII, 27r–v.

30. Ibid., 27v–28r.
31. The text of the decree can be found in ACDF, Index, Protocolli PP, 576r.
32. ACDF, Index, Diarii VII, September 7, 1670, 29v.
33. ACDF, Index, Protocolli PP, 280r.
34. ACDF, Index, Diarii VII, November 19, 1670, 30v.
35. ACDF, Index, Protocolli PP, 292r.
36. ACDF, Index, Diarii VII, November 23, 1671, 34v.

Chapter 8

1. ACDF, St St I 3 e, 1v–2v.
2. Ibid., 15r–28v at 15r.
3. Ibid., 15r–v.
4. Ibid., 19v–21r.
5. Ibid., 22r–23v.
6. Ibid., 24v–25v.
7. Serista's document can be found in Ibid., 31v–42v.
8. ACDF, SO Decreta 1674, January 11, 14r–v.
9. Ibid., February 28, 57r.
10. Ibid., July 25, 235r.
11. Ibid., August 29, 264v; September 5, 276r; October 24, 319r; and November 7, 335r.
12. The documents pertaining to this discussion can be found in ACDF, St St H 6 b, 373r and ff. (at 542r–571v we can find copies of the documents pertaining to Antonio's crime). The text of the final decree can be found in ACDF, SO Decreta 1676, October 22, 219v–220r. Pope Innocent XI used this decree as the basis for an Apostolic constitution, which was promulgated on March 12, 1677; the text can be found in *Bullarium Romanum*, vol. XIX (Turin, 1870), 41–43.
13. ACDF, SO Decreta 1678, March 8, 39v.
14. ACDF, SO Decreta 1679, March 22, 62v.
15. Ibid., April 19, 84v–85r.
16. ACDF, SO Decreta 1680, January 31, 23v.
17. Ibid., May 29, 110v–111r.
18. The documents pertaining to Miceli's trial can be found in ACDF, St St B 4 h, folder n.18. The text of the final decree can be found in ACDF, SO Decreta 1680, 132v–133r.
19. ACDF, SO Decreta 1680, August 21, 170v–171r.

20. ACDF, SO Decreta 1680, October 2, 209v, and ACDF, SO Decreta 1681, January 15, 11r.

21. See AAV, Segreteria di Stato, Napoli 90, 753r–754r, for the nuncio's updates on the latest negative developments of Carlo's career.

22. Bernardo de' Dominici, *Vita del Cavaliere D. Luca Giordano* (Naples, 1729), 49–51.

23. Ibid., 51.

24. Ibid.

25. ACDF, St St B 4 h, folder n.1, 252r–253r.

26. Ibid., 276r–294t at 277r.

27. Ibid., 293r–v.

28. ACDF, SO Decreta 1681, March 5, 45r.

Bibliographical Notes

Note on the Primary Sources

Generally speaking, documents related to canonizations can be found in the Archive of the Congregation of Rites and Ceremonies (instituted by Pope Sixtus V in 1588 with the aim of centralizing the process of saint-making and putting it under the exclusive control of the Roman authority), which today is housed in the Archivio Apostolico Vaticano. The Congregation of the Inquisition was usually involved in investigating suspicious cases of holiness, that is, cases in which the (usually local, but often even Roman) authorities suspected that the holy people in question were "feigned," "affected," or "pretended" saints, because of ignorance or self-delusion, or in order to take advantage of the credulity of their community for personal gain, or as a consequence of some heretical belief. In addition, again generally speaking, whenever the Roman authorities wanted to take a closer look at published or unpublished books narrating the deeds of saints (both official and unofficial), they called upon the Congregation of the Index of Prohibited Books, which was the institutional body in charge of examining and censoring books and manuscripts. Today, the archives of both the Roman Inquisition and the Index are housed in the Archive of the Congregation for the Doctrine of Faith, in Vatican City. Concerning the Inquisitorial activities in the Italian peninsula, we should also remember that local tribunals maintained their own archives in addition to the Roman one. In the case of Giovanni and Carlo Calà, the relevant local tribunal would be the one in Naples, and the records of the Neapolitan Holy Office can be found in the Archivio Storico Diocesano of Naples.

For an introduction (in English) to the history, nature, scope, and sources of the archives of the Inquisition and Index, I recommend the works of Christopher F. Black (especially *The Italian Inquisition*, New Haven: Yale University Press, 2009), Thomas F. Mayer (especially *The Roman Inquisition: A Papal Bureaucracy and Its Laws in the Age of Galileo*, Philadelphia: University of Pennsylvania Press, 2013), Peter Godman (especially *The Saint as Censor. Robert Bellarmine between Inquisition and Index*, Leiden: Brill, 2000), and John Tedeschi (especially *The Prosecution of Heresy: Collected Studies on the Inquisition in Early Modern Italy* (Binghamton, NY: Medieval and Renaissance Texts and Studies, 1991), and the collected volume he edited together with

Gustav Henningsen, *The Inquisition in Early Modern Europe: Studies on Sources and Methods* (DeKalb: Northern Illinois University Press, 1986). Additional references on the Inquisition are provided below, and especially in the bibliographical note on chapter 5.

Coming more specifically to the nature and provenance of the sources I used in this book, since, as it turned out pretty quickly, not only was Giovanni a fake saint, but he wasn't even a real person, no official canonization process was ever initiated (and thus, no records of Giovanni's case can be found among the canonization trials), and no accusation of feigned sanctity against him was ever brought. The one person on whom the attention of the Catholic authorities concentrated was Carlo Calà Duke of Diano, Giovanni's unquestionably real seventeenth-century successor, who not only promoted the cult of Giovanni within the kingdom of Naples, but also wrote books publicizing Giovanni's life and allegedly supernatural deeds. Consequently, the sources concerning the Calà case can be found in the records of both the Inquisition and the Index.

As far as I can tell, the Neapolitan archive of the Holy Office does not seem to contain any significant material on the case of Carlo and Giovanni Calà (although the Neapolitan archive does contain interesting documents related to the context in which the story unfolded). The reason for this, I believe, might be twofold. On the one hand, given the stature of Carlo Calà within the viceregal administration, and given the deep involvement of the Roman authorities in the case from early on, it is highly likely that the Neapolitan *ministro* and the archbishop of Naples would have made as much effort as possible to transfer all documents to Rome, so as to keep their Roman superior abreast of all the developments. On the other hand, I should also say that unlike the Roman archive, the section of the Neapolitan Archivio Diocesano that includes the documents related to the Neapolitan Inquisition is still in large part uncatalogued and not entirely available to scholars, especially in its seventeenth-century components. Therefore I cannot exclude that some document about the Calà case might turn up in the future. For useful information concerning the status of this archive, as well as for a thorough and informative inventory of what we do have, see Giovanni Romeo, "Il Fondo 'Sant'Ufficio' dell'Archivio Storico Diocesano di Napoli. Inventario (1549–1647)," special monographic issue of *Campania Sacra*, 34 (2003); for an English introduction to the sources related to early modern Naples, see John A. Marino, "Constructing the Past of Early Modern Naples: Sources and Historiography," in *A Companion to Early Modern Naples*, ed. Tommaso Astarita (Leiden: Brill, 2013), 11–34.

Even though I couldn't find significant sources on the case of Giovanni and Carlo Calà in Naples, the documentary material coming from the Roman archive of the Inquisition and Index is abundant, if scattered across a diverse set of sources. In general, we should remember that all the discussions, decisions, and supplementary documents related to the procedures of the Roman

Inquisition are collected in the folders named *Stanza Storica*, while all the documents pertaining to the examination and censure of books can be found under the rubric of *Protocolli*. Since both the duke and his books were subject to lengthy, thorough, and complex investigations, we have ample folders devoted to them among both the *Stanza Storica* and the *Protocolli*. But it is important to keep in mind that even though both sets of documents are rich, detailed, and wonderfully eye-opening, they only preserve a specific part (albeit crucial) of the story, giving very few hints as to what happened before or after the investigation and the larger context in which the investigation was carried out. In fact, aside from the specific case of the prophet Giovanni and indeed regardless of the specific topic we are interested in studying, from the documents preserved in either the *Stanza Storica* (if we are dealing with an Inquisition case) or the *Protocolli* (if we are dealing with a book or manuscript examined by the Index), we will certainly get a most valuable and well-defined snapshot, but we are left with no album in which we can put this photo alongside the others so as to get a sense of the development of the story and of how this story fits in the larger picture. As I always tell my students, imagine a wedding album containing only one single picture: a portrait of the bride and the groom. To be sure, a wedding portrait can provide valuable information. If we pay close attention to the faces and expressions, we might guess the age of the couple and get an idea of the conditions under which the picture was taken (Were they young or old? Did they seem to be posing? Did they seem relaxed?). If we look at the wedding gown and hairdos, we might get some clues as to the time and place (to remain within the Western tradition, a short A-line dress, for instance, might point to the late 1960s or early 1970s, while the strong shoulders and puffy sleeves might be markers of the 1980s). Other details of the jewelry, the shoes, or the quality of the picture might tell us something about the socio-economic status of the couple. Yet without seeing the location, it is impossible to tell where exactly the wedding took place and what kind of religious or secular ceremony it was. Without seeing pictures of the rest of the participants, it is impossible to know the size and composition of the wedding party, not to mention all the information concerning the larger cultural, social, and economic context that we would be missing if it weren't for the group shots.

Thus, with few (if any) exception, all the documents in the *Stanza Storica* and the *Protocolli* need to be supplemented. As far as the Roman Inquisition is concerned, the best place to start is the *Decreta* of the Holy Office. Simultaneously feared, revered, and hated by scholars, the *Decreta* are the minutes of the weekly meeting of the Congregation of the Inquisition. Organized by calendar years (systematically starting from about the early 1570s), the *Decreta* are rather peculiar sources, at once detailed and scant.

The compiler of the *Decreta* duly recorded who was present for each meeting, when and where the meeting took place, and all the cases that were discussed—of course, not all information is free of errors and sometimes (relatively rarely, actually) the decision taken on a particular case was not recorded, either because the record-keeper did not want to put in writing whatever the Cardinals said (especially if the trial involved high-profile defendants or extremely sensitive matters), or because the copyist was sloppy and made a mistake. Nevertheless, what we do have is pretty extensive. In fact, just to give a quantitative measure of how meticulously were these documents produced, I will say that each quarto volume covering a single year runs around (and in many cases longer than) 1,000 pages. Incidentally, we should remember that since the beginning of the 1590s, the Congregation of the Index also began keeping records of its meetings, now collected in volumes known as *Diarii,* but the Index minutes are much more condensed and less detailed than the corresponding Inquisition record, and in fact even though each volume of the *Diarii* covers multiple years, it is much shorter than the average volume of the *Decreta.*

Even though the vast majority of the topics discussed by the Inquisitors are recorded in the *Decreta,* each of these topic is mentioned in no more than a short phrase or two, summarizing briefly what the problem was and what the Inquisitors decided (or failed to decide) to do about it. In addition, even though most volumes of *Decreta* do contain an alphabetical index in which the reader might look for the names of the people whose cases the Inquisitors discussed with the relevant page numbers, in reality those indexes are far from inclusive and actually neglect more information than they record, so that, for the purpose of research, they are effectively useless.

For all these reasons, in order to follow a story through the *Decreta,* it is necessary to carefully read through an immense amount of pages spanning several volumes, given that usually even seemingly small problems were discussed over a period of several months, and often years, with only a short note marking what happened in each instance. In addition to the sheer length of the *Decreta,* to how labor-intensive it is to go through them, and to the problems arising from the specific kind of information that they preserve or omit, the rhetorical genre of these documents (which are akin, as I said, to the minutes one could read from, say, a faculty meeting), at first glance is not exactly enticing, let alone exciting. Yet, once one takes the plunge and dives in, it is nearly impossible to give up reading: behind the mindlessly dull bureaucratic language, there are innumerable stories of different people, issues, and contexts. These range from large-scope European-wide crises such as, in the central decades of the seventeenth century, the conflict over Jansenism, to small-time cases of regular people going on about their lives in their communities who at some point got caught in their own personal doctrinal drama and whose conflict with the Holy Office had no effects on the larger religious, theological, or political debates, even though it left an indelible trace, one way or another, in their own life and in that of their families and neighbors.

In addition to giving a sort of rough outline of how a case developed, the *Decreta* will also point to various links and ramifications between the case that we study and some other issue, which initially we wouldn't have expected to be related but which the records suggest that it was. For instance, the cardinals of the Holy Office might have referred to somebody else in their discussion of our case, or the local Inquisitor might have mentioned another problem or person while discussing the issue we have been following. Sometimes, simply seeing our case being discussed at the same meeting as another case might make us think of our problem in a completely different light and might suggest possible avenues for research that we hadn't thought about before (and while I cannot stress to my own students strongly enough the need to go to the archives well prepared, at the same time I also tell them to expect, cultivate, and cherish those serendipitous changes of direction). Thus, reading the *Decreta* (and reading the *Diarii*, the much more condensed collections of the minutes of the Index) means accepting their invitation to follow up on those links, either by searching back within the records of the Inquisition and Index, or by searching in other archives and libraries (and normally by doing both). Whatever we find as a follow-up to our original question might, in turn, lead us back to the *Decreta* (or to another kind of source), and the cycle begins all over again until we find that no new leads emerge and/or we decide that what we did find is enough for our purpose.

To be sure, not all leads take somewhere, and sometimes we are forced to admit that one or two short references to some person or issue in the *Decreta* or the *Diarii* is the only record we are ever going to find about that person or that issue, and thus the trail goes cold (and I use this investigative metaphor consciously, as anybody familiar with Carlo Ginzburg's scholarship will have already noted). By personal experience, I can say that usually, if we search we will find something, which means that we will certainly learn something we didn't know before, but also that there is always going to be something we will miss.

The procedure I just sketched mirrors the one I followed in researching this book. I was going through the *Decreta* looking for something else, and then I began to notice the references to the Calà case. Intrigued by this story, I systematically studied the *Decreta* to get a rough idea of how it unfolded. Then I was lucky enough to find more specific information in the *Stanza Storica* and *Protocolli*, which contain extensive documents on the investigation launched by the Inquisition and Index. Afterward, I went back to the *Decreta* and the *Diarii*, this time in order to notice links, ramifications, and connections. As the readers have seen, the Calà case turned out to be connected to several questions and issues, on which I followed up with different kinds of sources, both printed and in manuscript form, in other archives and libraries, and specifically in the Archivio Diocesano in Naples, the Vatican Library, the Archivio Apostolico Vaticano, and the Jesuit archives. When I felt that the cycle was no longer producing new leads but had instead started to twist around upon itself, I stopped. I know that I learned a lot, but I also know that there is something I missed. I know that I could always do better (and other scholars who might want to take up this topic in the future will certainly move forward), but I also know that no matter how hard we try, we will always miss something. All in all, I believe that I have managed to uncover what I thought were the most important aspects of this story, and I am confident that my interpretation is coherent, correct, and provisionally true.

Introduction

For an introduction to Momigliano's thoughts on history and historiography, I would recommend starting from the essays collected in *Studies in Historiography* (London: Weidenfeld and Nicolson, 1966), as well as *The Classical Foundations of Modern Historiography* (Berkeley: University of California Press, 1990). On forgeries and, more generally, the cultural role of erudition in early modern Europe, see the seminal work of Anthony Grafton and, in particular, *Joseph Scaliger: A Study in the History of Classical Scholarship*, vol. I, *Textual Criticism and Exegesis* (Oxford: Oxford University Press, 1983); *Joseph Scaliger: A Study in the History of Classical Scholarship*, vol. II, *Historical Chronology* (Oxford: Oxford University Press, 1994); *Forgers and Critics: Creativity and Duplicity in Western Scholarship* (Princeton: Princeton University Press, 1990); *Defenders of the Text: The Traditions of Scholarship in an Age of Science, 1450–1800* (Cambridge, MA: Harvard University Press, 1991); *The Footnote: A Curious History* (Cambridge, MA: Harvard University Press, 1997); and *Worlds Made by Words: Scholarship and Community in the Modern West* (Cambridge, MA: Harvard University Press, 2009). On the place of erudition in the development of the historical method see also Grafton, *What Was History? The Art of History in Early Modern Europe* (Cambridge: Cambridge University Press, 2007).

For the relationship between theology, religion, and historical and documentary criticism see, among others, Nicholas Hardy, *Criticism and Confession. The Bible in the Seventeenth-Century Republic of Letters* (Oxford: Oxford University Press, 2017); Jean-Louis Quantin, *The Church of England and Christian Antiquity. The Construction of a Confessional Identity in the 17th Century* (Oxford: Oxford University Press, 2009), and "Reason and Reasonableness in French Ecclesiastical Scholarship," *Huntington Library Quarterly,* 74 (2011): 401–436; Katherine Van Liere, Simon Ditchfield, and Howard Louthan, eds., *Sacred History. Uses of the Christian Past in the Renaissance World* (Oxford: Oxford University Press, 2012); Anthony Grafton and Joanna Weinberg. *"I Have Always Loved the Holy Tongue": Isaac Casaubon, the Jews, and a Forgotten Chapter in Renaissance Scholarship*

(Cambridge, MA: Harvard University Press, 2011); and the work of Simon Ditchfield, starting with *Liturgy, Sanctity, and History in Tridentine Italy. Pietro Maria Campi and the Preservation of the Particular* (Cambridge: Cambridge University Press, 1995). On the role of documentary accuracy and historical authenticity in the process of saint-making, see the references I give in the bibliographical note on chapter 2.

Carlo Ginzburg's *The Cheese and the Worms,* English trans. by John Tedeschi and Anne Tedeschi (Baltimore, The Johns Hopkins University Press, 1980); Natalie Zemon Davis's *The Return of Martin Guerre* (Cambridge, MA: Harvard University Press, 1982); and Giovanni Levi's *Inheriting Power: The Story of an Exorcist,* English trans. by Lydia G. Cochrane (Chicago: The University of Chicago Press, 1988) are usually considered the pioneering works in the field of microhistory. Ginzburg and Levi have also written extensively on the methodological, ideological, and cultural nature of microhistory. Among the works available in English, see especially Levi's "On Microhistory," in Peter Burke, ed., *New Perspectives on Historical Writing* (University Park: The Pennsylvania State University Press, 1992), 93–113, and Ginzburg's *Clues, Myths, and the Historical Method,* English trans. by John Tedeschi and Anne Tedeschi (Baltimore, The Johns Hopkins University Press, 1989); *History, Rhetoric, and Proof* (Hanover: University Press of New England, 1999); and *Threads and Traces: True False Fictive,* English trans. by Anne C. Tedeschi and John Tedeschi (Berkeley: University of California Press, 2012). This latter work includes the English translation of Ginzburg's postscript to the Italian translation of Natalie Zemon Davis's *The Return of Martin Guerre,* from which I quoted. Siegfried Kracauer's *History. The Last Things Before the Last* (Oxford: Oxford University Press, 1969) contains thought-provoking reflections on questions of scale and perspective. The image of the microhistorian as a truffle hunter (as opposed to the macrohistorian as a parachutist) comes from Emmanuel Le Roy Ladurie, *Paris-Montpellier. P.C.-P.S.U. 1945–1963* (Paris: Gallimard, 1982). In *The Historian's Craft* (English trans. by Peter Putnam (New York: Alfred A. Knopf, 1954)), Marc Bloch has compared the historian's attitude toward documents to the attraction that the "ogre of the fairy tale" feels when catching "the scent of human flesh." Edoardo Grendi wrote about an extra-ordinary document that could turn out to be *"eccezionalmente 'normale'"* (exceptionally normal) in "Micro-analisi e storia sociale," *Quaderni Storici* 35 (1977): 506–520.

For a sample of the debate concerning the role that microhistory can or should play in the current historiographical context and especially with respect to the growing interest for world history and global approaches, see John Brewer, "Microhistory and the Histories of Everyday Life," *Cultural and Social History,* 7 (2010): 87–109 with Filippo de Vivo's reply: "Prospect or Refuge: Microhistory, History on the Large Scale—a Response," *Cultural and Social History,* 7 (2010): 387–397; Francesca Trivellato, "Microstoria, storia del mondo, e storia globale," in *A Venticinque Anni da "L'eredità immateriale*," ed. Paola Lanaro (Milan: Franco Angeli, 2011), 119–131 (which contains the anecdote about Giovanni Levi and the squeezing of sources that I mentioned) and "Is There a Future for Italian Microhistory in the Age of Global History?" *California Italian Studies* 2 (2011), https://escholarship.org/uc/item/0z94n9hq; Thomas V. Cohen, "The Macrohistory of Microhistory," *Journal of Medieval and Early Modern Studies* 47 (2017): 53–73. My reference to the democratization of history comes from Lynn Hunt, *History. Why It Matters* (Medford, MA: Polity Press, 2018).

Chapter 1

For a synthetic and accessible overview of the history of the kingdom of Naples from antiquity to modern times see Tommaso Astarita, *Between Salt Water and Holy Water. A History of Southern Italy* (London: W.W. Norton, 2005). For a scholarly introduction to selected themes in the social, political, religious, and cultural history of early modern Naples see Astarita, ed., *A Companion to Early Modern Naples*. For an introduction to the main political, economic, social, and religious aspects of the Calabria region see Giuseppe Galasso, *La Calabria Spagnola* (Milan: Rubettino, 2012). For a synthetic biographical sketch of Carlo Calà see Aldo Mazzacane's entry devoted to him in the *Dizionario Biografico degli Italiani*.

On the political, social, and economic history of early modern Naples the work of Giuseppe Galasso is still a fundamental reference point: among others, see *Alla Periferia dell'Impero. Il Regno di Napoli nel Periodo Spagnolo (secoli XVI–XVII)* (Turin: Einaudi, 1994); *Napoli Spagnola dopo Masaniello: Politica, Cultura, Società*, 2 vols. (Florence: Sansoni, 1982); and Galasso's edited volumes on the kingdom of Naples in *Storia d'Italia, Il Regno di Napoli* (Turin: Einaudi, 2005–2011). Also important for understanding the relationship between the kingdom of Naples and the Spanish crown are Aurelio Musi's works, starting with *Mezzogiorno Spagnolo: la Via Napoletana allo Stato Moderno* (Naples: Guida, 1991), *L'Italia dei Viceré. Integrazione e Resistenza nel Sistema Imperiale Spagnolo* (Cava de' Tirreni: Avagliano, 2000), as well as his edited volume *Nel Sistema Imperiale: l'Italia Spagnola* (Naples: Guida, 1994).

On the role of the feudal nobility and its relationship with the Spanish absolutist government see also Tommaso Astarita, *The Continuity of Feudal Power. The Caracciolo di Brienza in Spanish Naples* (Cambridge: Cambridge University Press, 1991); on the Neapolitan *togati* see Pier Luigi Rovito, *La Respublica dei Togati: Giuristi e Società nella Napoli del Seicento* (Naples: Jovene, 1981). On the economic, financial, and fiscal aspects of the history of the kingdom see also Aurelio Musi, "Fisco, Religione e Stato nel Mezzogiorno d'Italia (secoli XVI–XVII)," in *Fisco, Religione, Stato nell'Età Confessionale*, ed.

Paolo Prodi and Hermann Kellenbenz (Bologna: Il Mulino, 1999), 427–457; Luigi de Rosa, *Il Mezzogiorno Spagnolo tra Crescita e Decadenza* (Bari: Laterza, 1999); Giovanni Muto, *Le Finanze Pubbliche Napoletane tra Riforma e Restaurazione, 1520–1634* (Naples: Edizioni Scientifiche Italiane, 1980), and *Saggi sul Governo dell'Economia nel Mezzogiorno Spagnolo* (Naples: Edizioni Scientifiche Italiane, 1992); and, in English, Antonio Calabria, *The Cost of Empire. The Finances of the Kingdom of Naples in the Time of the Spanish Rule* (Cambridge: Cambridge University Press, 1991).

On Masaniello's revolt there is an abundant biography. To begin with, see the classic (and complementary) interpretations by Rosario Villari, *The Revolt of Naples* (Cambridge: Cambridge University Press, 1993, first Italian ed. 1967), and Peter Burke, "The Virgin of the Carmine and the Revolt of Masaniello," *Past and Present* 99 (1983): 3–21.

For more information on the political, social, and cultural role that public festivals played in early modern Naples see, among others, John A. Marino, *Becoming Neapolitan: Citizen Culture in Baroque Naples* (Baltimore: The Johns Hopkins University Press, 2010), and Gabriel Guarino, *Representing the King's Splendour: Communication and Reception of Symbolic Forms of Power in Viceregal Naples* (Manchester: Manchester University Press, 2010).

On the anti-clerical arguments elaborated by Carlo Calà and his fellow Neapolitan jurists see Agostino Lauro, *Il Giurisdizionalismo Pregiannoniano nel Regno di Napoli* (Rome: Edizioni di Storia e Letteratura, 1974). On the political and theological repercussions of the debates on clerical exemption see Vittorio Frajese, "Regno Ecclesiastico e Stato Moderno. La Polemica fra Francisco Peña e Roberto Bellarmino sull'Esenzione dei Clerici," *Annali dell'Istituto Storico Italo-Germanico in Trento* 14 (1988): 273–339, and Stefania Tutino, *Empire of Souls. Robert Bellarmine and the Christian Commonwealth* (Oxford: Oxford University Press, 2010), ch. 3.

The figures I give concerning the value of the fief of Diano and its corresponding title (as well as all other estimates presented in this book) are based on the estimates of the value of money, wages, and cost of living in early modern Rome provided by Franco Mormando in *Bernini: His Life and His Rome* (Chicago: The University of Chicago Press, 2011). Mormando's estimates are given in *scudi*, which were the standard currency in Rome. As far as the Kingdom of Naples was concerned, the standard currency was the *ducato*, whose value, in the seventeenth century, was slightly lower than that of the Roman *scudo* (although of course we must take into account the occasional and in many cases dramatic fluctuations and devaluations, which in seventeenth-century Naples were rather frequent, caused by either natural calamities or fiscal and financial crisis). For more information on how the early modern Curia understood the relationship between the value of Neapolitan *ducati* and that of Roman *scudi* when it had to calculate the exchange rate of the pensions granted to cardinals, bishops, and other papal officers, see

Mario Rosa, "Curia Romana e pensioni ecclesiastiche: fiscalità pontificia nel Mezzogiorno (secoli XVI–XVIII)," *Quaderni Storici* 14 (1979): 1015–1055.

For an overview of the political and cultural role that genealogies (both real and fictive) played in early modern Europe see Roberto Bizzocchi, *Genealogie Incredibili. Scritti di Storia nell'Europa Moderna* (Bologna: Il Mulino, 1995). On Annius of Viterbo and, more generally, on the importance of forgeries in the development of Western scholarship and in the cultural and intellectual history of Europe see Anthony Grafton's works, and especially "Invention of Tradition and Traditions of Invention in Renaissance Europe: The Strange Case of Annius of Viterbo," in *The Transmission of Culture in Early Modern Europe*, ed. Anthony Grafton and Ann Blair (Philadelphia: University of Pennsylvania Press, 1990), 8–38; *Forgers and Critics*; and *Defenders of the Text*.

Scholarship on the religious, liturgical, and devotional history of early modern Naples is steadily growing. On the attempt on the part of the post-Tridentine authorities to control popular devotion in the kingdom of Naples see Elisa Novi Chavarria, *Il Governo delle Anime. Azione Pastorale, Predicazione e Missioni nel Mezzogiorno d'Italia. Secoli XVI–XVIII* (Naples: Editoriale Scientifica, 2001). On the Jesuits' missionary efforts in the kingdom of Naples see Jennifer D. Selwyn, *A Paradise Inhabited by Devils. The Jesuits' Civilizing Mission in Early Modern Naples* (Farnham: Ashgate, 2004). On the role of gender in the religious life of the city, and on some distinctively interesting case studies, see Paola Zito, *Giulia e l'Inquisitore. Simulazione di Santità e Misticismo nella Napoli di Primo Seicento* (Naples: Arte Tipografica, 2000); Elisa Novi Chavarria, *Monache e Gentildonne. Un Labile Confine. Poteri Politici e Identità Religiose nei Monasteri Napoletani. Secoli XVI–XVII* (Milan: Angeli, 2001); Helen Hills, *Invisible City. The Architecture of Devotion in Seventeenth-Century Neapolitan Convents*, Oxford: (Oxford University Press, 2004). On religious festivities and the religious and devotional dimensions of public festivals, in addition to the already-mentioned works by Burke, Marino, and Guarino, see Edward Muir, "The Virgin on the Street Corner: the Place of the Sacred in Italian Cities, in *Religion and Culture in the Renaissance and Reformation*, ed. Steven Ozment (Kirksville, MO: Sixteenth Century Journal Publisher, 1989), 25–40; Maria Antonietta Visceglia, "Rituali Religiosi e Gerarchie Politiche a Napoli in Età Moderna," in *Fra Storia e Storiografia: Scritti in Onore di Pasquale Villani*, ed. Paolo Macry and Angelo Massafra (Bologna: Il Mulino, 1994), 587–620.

For an overview of the cults of saints in Naples see Jean-Michel Sallmann, *Naples et Ses Saints à l'Âge Baroque (1540–1750)*, (Paris: Presses Universitaires de France, 1994). San Gennaro and the ceremonies held in his honor have been the object of an increasing attention on the part of historians, art historians, and musicologists. For a starting point on the historical sources concerning San Gennaro and his cult in early modern Naples, see Gennaro Luongo, ed., *San Gennaro nel XVII Centenario del Martirio (305–2005)*, 2 vols. (Naples: ECS, 2007). For a few suggestive reflections concerning the cultural relevance of San Gennaro's blood and the chapel in which it is preserved, see Helen Hills, *The Matter of Miracles. Neapolitan Baroque Architecture & Sanctity* (Manchester: Manchester University Press, 2016). For an account of the numerous explanations proposed for the miracle of the liquefaction of San Gennaro's blood from the Middle Ages up to the present times, see Francesco Paolo de Ceglia, *Il Segreto di San Gennaro. Storia naturale di un miracolo napoletano* (Turin: Einaudi, 2016).

Concerning the quantitative dimensions of the Neapolitan secular clergy, reliable and valuable data can be found in Giuseppe Galasso and Carla Russo, eds., *Per la Storia Sociale del Mezzogiorno*, 2 vols. (Naples: Guida, 1980). On the role of the papal nuncios in the institutional and political context of the Curia, it is still fundamental Paolo Prodi, *The Papal Prince. One Body and Two Souls: The Papal Monarchy in Early Modern Europe* (Cambridge: Cambridge University Press, 1987, first Italian ed. 1982). On the history of the Inquisition in Naples, see Luigi Amabile, *Il Santo Officio della Inquisizione in Napoli. Narrazione con Molti Documenti Inediti*, 2 vols. (Città di Castello: Lapi, 1892, reprinted in 1987 by Rubettino, Milan). Despite the fact that Amabile wrote well before the archives of the Roman Inquisition were open to the public, his account is remarkably accurate, and therefore it is still a useful starting point. For a more recent analysis of the theological, political, and ecclesiological characteristics of the Inquisition in Naples see also Giovanni Romeo's works, starting with "Per la Storia del Sant'Ufficio a Napoli tra '500 e '600. Documenti e Problemi," *Campania Sacra*, 7 (1976): 5–109, and "Una città, Due Inquisizioni: l'Anomalia del Sant'Ufficio a Napoli nel Tardo '500," *Rivista di Storia e Letteratura Religiosa*, 24 (1988): 42–67. On the specificities of the Inquisitorial activities in Naples in a comparative perspective see Adriano Prosperi, "Per la Storia dell'Inquisizione Romana," in Adriano Prosperi, *L'Inquisizione Romana. Letture e Ricerche* (Rome: Edizioni di Storia e Letteratura, 2003), 29–68. On the financial, fiscal, and economic difficulties of the Neapolitan tribunal of the Holy Office, and for more information on the costs that the Inquisitors incurred in order to maintain their prisoners, see Germano Maifreda, *The Business of the Roman Inquisition in the Early Modern Era* (London: Routledge, 2017, first Italian ed. 2014). For a background on the political and jurisdictional conflict between the Inquisition and the viceregal government see also Thomas F. Mayer's work, and especially *The Roman Inquisition on the Stage of Italy, c.1590–1640* (Philadelphia: University of Pennsylvania Press, 2014), especially chaps.1 and 2.

Chapter 2

By the very end of the seventeenth century, Stocchi's forgery had been fully exposed, and between the eighteenth and the twentieth centuries, a handful of authors reported the story of the Duke of Diano and his fake ancestor Giovanni (to varying degrees of historical precision). Among the available accounts, see the relatively accurate book published by the scholar and antiquarian Paolo Antonio Paoli OMD, in *Notizie spettanti all'opera apocrifa intitolata "Storia degli Svevi"* (Rome, 1792). For a more recent account, see Domenico Zangari, *Di Carlo Calà e Ferdinando Stocchi. Cenno sulla famosa falsificazione della "Storia degli Svevi" nella conquista del Regno di Napoli"* (Naples, 1921). See also the entry devoted to Stocchi in Louis Gabriel Michaud's *Biographie universelle ancienne et moderne* (Paris, 1811–1828), s.v. "Stocchi, Ferdinand." I have explored some of the elements of this story in "The Case of Carlo Calà and Giovanni Calà: Historical Truth and Doctrinal Orthodoxy in Post-Reformation Italy," *Erudition and the Republic of Letters,* 1 (2016): 412–463.

The bibliography on the evolution of the process of saint-making in post-Tridentine Catholicism is quite extensive. For an overview see Simon Ditchfield, "Tridentine Worship and the Cult of Saints," in *The Cambridge History of Christianity,* ed. Ronnie Po-Chia Hsia (Cambridge: Cambridge University Press, 2007), vol. VI, 201–224, and Clare Copeland, "Sanctity," in *The Ashgate Research Companion to the Counter-Reformation,* ed. Alexandra Bamji, Geert H. Janssen, and Mary Laven (Farnham: Ashgate, 2013), 225–241. See also Peter Burke, "How to become a Counter-Reformation Saint," in *Religion and Society in Early Modern Europe, 1500–1800,* ed. Kaspar von Greyerz (London: German Historical Institute, 1984), 45–55; Gabriella Zarri, *Le Sante Vive: Cultura e Religiosità Femminile nella Prima Età Moderna* (Turin: Rosenberg & Sellier, 1990), and Gabriella Zarri, ed., *Finzione e Santità tra Medioevo ed Età Moderna* (Turin: Roseberg & Sellier, 1991); Simon Ditchfield, "How Not to be a Counter-Reformation Saint: The Attempted Canonization of Pope Gregory IX, 1622–45," *Papers of the British School at Rome* 60 (1992): 379–422; "Sanctity in Early Modern History," *Journal of Ecclesiastical History* 47 (1996): 98–122; and "Thinking with Saints: Sanctity and Society in the Early Modern World," *Critical Inquiry* 35 (2009): 552–584; Clare Copeland, *Maria Maddalena de' Pazzi. The Making of a Counter-Reformation Saint* (Oxford: Oxford University Press, 2016). Urban VIII's decrees concerning saints and canonization procedures were published in the collection *Urbani VIII P. O. M. Decreta Servanda in Canonizatione et Beatificatione Sanctorum* (Rome, 1642). On the juridical developments of the process of canonization in the seventeenth and eighteenth centuries see Giuseppe Della Torre, "Santità ed Economia Processuale. L'esperienza giuridica da Urbano VIII a Benedetto XIV," in *Finzione e Santità,* 231–263. On the Pope's policy concerning canonizations see Miguel Gotor, *I Beati del Papa* (Florence: Olschki, 2002).

On the role that historical accuracy and documentary authenticity played in the process of saint-making see, among others, Adriano Prosperi, "L'Elemento Storico nelle Polemiche Sulla Santità," in *Finzione e Santità,* ed. Gabriella Zarri, 88–119; Anthony Grafton, *Defenders of the Text, the Footnote: A Curious History,* and *Worlds Made by Words*; Simon Ditchfield, *Liturgy, Sanctity, and History*; Jean-Louis Quantin "Reason and Reasonableness"; Katherine Van Liere, Simon Ditchfield, and Howard Louthan, eds., *Sacred History*; Katrina B. Olds, *Forging the Past: Invented Histories in Counter-Reformation Spain* (New Haven: Yale University Press, 2015)). On the tension between historical authenticity and doctrinal truth see also Tutino, "'For the Sake of the Truth of History and of the Catholic Doctrines': History, Documents, and Dogma in Cesare Baronio's *Annales Ecclesiastici,*" *Journal of Early Modern History* 17 (2013): 125–159. As a general background on the relationship between the truth of history and the truth of theology see Arnaldo Momigliano, "The Origins of Ecclesiastical Historiography," in Momigliano, *The Classical Foundations of Modern Historiography,* 132–152, and Carlo Ginzburg, *Threads and Traces.* For the role that forgeries played in the cultural and intellectual history of early modern Europe see Grafton's classic *Forgers and Critics,* as well as *Defenders of the Text.* For an especially fascinating case study see Ingrid D. Rowland, *The Scarith of Scornello: A Tale of Renaissance Forgery* (Chicago: The University of Chicago Press, 2004). On literary forgery see also Walter Stephens, Earle Havens, and Janet Gonez, eds., *Literary Forgery in Early Modern Europe, 1450–1800* (Baltimore: The Johns Hopkins University Press, 2019). On early modern impostors see also Miriam Eliav-Feldon, *Renaissance Impostors and Proofs of Identity* (London: Palgrave Macmillan, 2012). On the epistemological challenges that the post-Tridentine Church faced when trying to establish the authenticity of allegedly miraculous events see Stuart Clark, *Vanities of the Eye. Vision in Early Modern European Culture* (Oxford: Oxford University Press, 2007), and Jan Machielsen and Clare Copeland, eds., *Angels of Light? Sanctity and the Discernment of Spirits in the Early Modern Period* (Leiden: Brill, 2012). On Novello de Bonis and, more generally, on the social, economic, political, and intellectual role of printers of hagiographies in early modern Naples see Sallmann, *Naples et Ses Saints.*

On the functions of notaries and notarized documents in early modern Italian society see Laurie Nussdorfer, *Brokers of Public Trust: Notaries in Early Modern Rome* (Baltimore: The Johns Hopkins University Press, 2009); Markus Friedrich, "Notarial Archives in the Papal States. Central Control and Local Histories of Record-Keeping in Early Modern Italy," *Mélanges de l'École Française de Rome* 123 (2011): 443–464; and *The Birth of the Archive. A History of Knowledge* (Ann Arbor: The University of Michigan Press, 2018, first German ed. 2011).

Chapter 3

On the impact of Mount Vesuvius on the larger cultural context of early modern Italy see Sean Cocco, *Watching Vesuvius. A History of Science and Culture in Early Modern Italy* (Chicago: The University of Chicago Press, 2013). Athanasius Kircher has recently been the object of a renewed scholarly interest, and the bibliography on the cultural and intellectual role he occupied in the erudite culture of his time is steadily growing. As a starting point, see the collection of essays edited by Paula Findlen, *Athanasius Kircher. The Last Man Who Knew Everything* (New York: Routledge, 2004), and Daniel Stolzenberg, *Egyptian Oedipus. Athanasius Kircher and the Secrets of Antiquity* (Chicago: The University of Chicago Press, 2013). On the wider cultural and intellectual implications of the early modern debate over giants see Jean Céard, "La querelle des géants et la jeunesse du monde," *Journal of Medieval and Renaissance Studies* 8 (1978): 37–76; Antoine Schnapper, "Persistance des géants," *Annales* 41 (1986): 177–200; and Paula Findlen, "Jokes of Nature and Jokes of Knowledge: the Playfulness of Scientific Discourse in Early Modern Europe," *Renaissance Quarterly* 43 (1990): 292–331. A stimulating study of the manifold significance of giants in the work of Rabelais is Walter Stephens, *Giants in Those Days: Folklore, Ancient History, and Nationalism* (Lincoln: University of Nebraska Press, 1989). On the relationship between Athanasius Kircher and Carlo Calà see Roberto Quirós Rosado, "Falsificación Genealógica y Filosofía Natural en el Nápoles Virreinal: la Red Epistolar de Athanasius Kircher y Carlo Calà (1661–1668)," in *En Tierra de Confluencias. Italia y la Monarquía de España, Siglos XVI-XVIII*, ed. Cristina Bravo Lozano and Roberto Quirós Rosado (Valencia: Albatros, 2013), 285–299.

Chapter 4

For a synthetic and relatively accessible account of Joachim of Fiore's life and works, as well as for an introduction to the main scholarly questions on his theology and spirituality, see Matthias Riedl, ed., *A Companion to Joachim of Fiore* (Leiden: Brill, 2017). On Joachim's thought and its impact in the religious, intellectual, and cultural history of Europe, Marjorie Reeves's works remain fundamental. Among them, see *Influence of Prophecy in the Later Middle Ages. A Study in Joachimism* (Oxford: Clarendon Press, 1969); *Joachim of Fiore and the Prophetic Future* (New York: Harper & Row, 1977); *The Prophetic Sense of History in Medieval and Renaissance Europe* (Farnham: Ashgate, 1999); and with Warwick Gould, *Joachim of Fiore and the Myth of the Eternal Evangel in the Nineteenth Century* (Oxford: Oxford University Press, 1987). For a study of the place of Joachim in a wider intellectual context see Bernard McGinn, *The Calabrian Abbot: Joachim of Fiore in the History of Western Thought* (New York:

Macmillan, 1985). On Joachim's theological thought see Antonio Crocco, *Gioacchino da Fiore* (Naples: Edizioni Empireo, 1960). For philologically accurate studies concerning the medieval and early modern sources on Joachim, see also Herbert Grundmann's works, and especially *Neue Forschungen über Joachim von Fiore* (Marburg: Simons, 1950), and "Zur Biographie Joachims von Fiore und Rainers von Ponza," *Deutsches Archiv für Erforschung des Mittelalters* 16 (1960): 137–546.

On the importance of Ughelli's *Italia Sacra* and, more generally, on the significance of local antiquarian research in the religious, cultural, and intellectual history of post-Tridentine Catholicism see Ditchfield, *Liturgy, Sanctity and History*. On the Bollandists see David Knowles, *Great Historical Enterprises: Problems in Monastic History* (Edinburgh: Thomas Nelson and Sons, 1963), 1–32 and Jan Machielsen, "Heretical Saints and Textual Discernment: the Polemical Origins of the *Acta Sanctorum* (1643–1940)," in *Angels of Light?*, 103–141.

Chapter 5

On credulity and credibility in early modern Catholic culture see Tutino, *The Many Faces of "Credulitas": Credibility, Credulity, and Belief in Post-Reformation Catholicism* (Oxford: Oxford University Press, forthcoming).

The institutional, political, legal, and procedural history of the Roman Inquisition has attracted remarkable scholarly attention in the last few decades. Among the many works available in English, see John Tedeschi, *The Prosecution of Heresy*, and *The Inquisition in Early Modern Europe*; Christopher F. Black, *The Italian Inquisition*; Thomas Mayer's three-volume series *The Roman Inquisition* (Philadelphia: University of Pennsylvania Press, 2012–2015); and Katherine Aron-Beller and Christopher F. Black, eds., *The Roman Inquisition: Centre vs. Peripheries* (Leiden: Brill, 2018). For scholarship in Italian, in addition to the already-mentioned works by Adriano Prosperi and Giovanni Romeo, see Prosperi, *Tribunali della Coscienza. Inquisitori, Confessori, Missionari* (Turin: Einaudi, 1996) and Andrea Dal Col, *L'Inquisizione in Italia dal XII al XXI Secolo* (Milan: Mondadori, 2006). On the Congregation of the Index and, more generally, on the process of censoring books in early modern Italy, see the trilogy by Gigliola Fragnito, *La Bibbia al Rogo. La Censura Ecclesiastica e i Volgarizzamenti della Scrittura (1471–1605)* (Bologna: Il Mulino, 1997), *Proibito Capire. La Chiesa e il Volgare nella Prima Età Moderna* (Bologna: Il Mulino, 2005), and *Rinascimento Perduto: la letteratura italiana sotto gli occhi dei censori (secoli XV–XVII)* (Bologna: Il Mulino, 2019); Vittorio Frajese, *Nascita dell'Indice: la Censura Ecclesiastica dal Rinascimento alla Controriforma* (Brescia: Morcelliana, 2006); Marco Cavarzere, *La Prassi della Censura nell'Italia del Seicento. Tra Repressione e Mediazione* (Rome:

Edizioni di Storia e Letteratura, 2011); and, in English, Paul F. Grendler, *The Roman Inquisition and the Venetian Press, 1540–1605* (Princeton: Princeton University Press, 1977); Peter Godman, *The Saint as Censor*; Giorgio Caravale, *Forbidden Prayer. Church Censorship and Devotional Literature in Renaissance Italy* (London: Routledge, 2016).

On Descartes's view of the Eucharist and its theological implications see Jean-Robert Armogathe's classic *Theologia Cartesiana: l'Explication Physique de l'Eucharistie chez Descartes et Dom Desgabets* (The Hague: Nijhoff, 1977), and Maria Pia Donato, "Scienza e Teologia nelle Congregazioni Romane. La Questione Atomista, 1626–1727," in *Rome et la Science Moderne: entre Renaissance et Lumières*, ed. Antonella Romano (Rome: École Française de Rome, 2008), 595–634.

Chapter 6

For a biography of Gradi see the excellent entry by Tomaso Montanari in the *DBI* and also Stjepan Krasič, *Stefano Gradič (1613–1683): Diplomatico e Prefetto della Biblioteca Apostolica Vaticana* (Rome: Pontificia Università Gregoriana, 1987). For a biography of Ricci see Francesco Bustaffa, "Michelangelo Ricci (1619–1682): Biografia di un cardinale innocenziano," unpublished Ph.D. thesis, Università degli Studi della Repubblica di San Marino, 2011. Early modern Italian academies and, more generally, the learned culture of early modern Italy have been the subject of a renewed scholarly interest at the intersection between the history and sociology of knowledge, the history of science, and the history of erudition. For some background on this scholarly approach, the work done by Ann Blair, Mordechai Feingold (especially his edited volumes on the history of universities), Paula Findlen, Anthony Grafton, Antonella Romano, and Pamela Smith is particularly important. Concerning early modern Italian academies more specifically, a good place to start is the online database developed by a team funded by the AHRC in the United Kingdom (https://www.bl.uk/catalogues/ItalianAcademies/About.aspx).

On the link between theology and erudition in Mabillon, see Jean-Louis Quantin, "Reason and Reasonableness." On the theological and cultural implications of the debate over the identity of the Pseudo-Dionysius see Jerry H. Bentley, *Humanists and Holy Writ. New Testament Scholarship in the Renaissance* (Princeton: Princeton University Press, 1983); John Monfasani, "Pseudo-Dionysius the Areopagite in mid-Quattrocento Rome," in *Supplementum Festivum: Studies in Honor of Paul Oskar Kristeller*, ed. James Hankins, John Monfasani, and Frederick Purnell Jr. (Binghamton: Medieval and Renaissance Texts and Studies, 1987), 189–219; and "Criticism of Biblical Humanists in Quattrocento Italy," in *Biblical Humanism and Scholasticism in the Age of Erasmus*, ed. Erika Rummel (Leiden: Brill, 2008), 15–38; Jean-Louis

Quantin, "The Fathers in Seventeenth-Century Roman Catholic Theology," in *The Reception of the Church Fathers in the West*, ed. Irena Backus (Leiden: Brill, 1997), 987–1008; Anthony Grafton, *Bring Out Your Dead. The Past as a Revelation* (Cambridge MA: Harvard University Press, 2001).

In the last few decades, scholars are focusing on the archive not simply as the privileged site for historical research, but rather as an object of historical inquiry in and of itself. For recent examples of this kind of scholarship see Ann M. Blair and Jennifer Milligan, eds., *Toward a Cultural History of Archives*, special issue of *Archival Science*, 7 (2007); Liesbeth Corens, Kate Peters, and Alexandra Walsham, eds., *The Social History of the Archive: Record Keeping in Early Modern Europe, Past & Present* Supplement 11 (2016); and *Archives and Information in the Early Modern World, Proceedings of the British Academy* (Oxford: Oxford University Press, 2018); Filippo de Vivo, Andrea Guidi, and Alessandro Silvestri, eds., *Archival Transformations in Early Modern European History*, special issue of *European History Quarterly*, 43 (2016). On the role that archives and, more generally, information management had on the political, social, religious, and cultural history of early modern Europe, see also Jacob Soll, *The Information Master. Jean-Baptiste Colbert's Secret State Intelligence System* (Ann Arbor: The University of Michigan Press, 2009); Anja-Silvia Goeing, *Storing, Archiving, Organizing: The Changing Dynamics of Scholarly Information Management in Post-Reformation Zurich* (Leiden: Brill, 2016); as well as the already-mentioned works by Markus Friedrich. On the epistemological, political, and intellectual issues at stake in the debate over the *ius archivii*, see Randolph C. Head, "Documents, Archives, and Proof around 1700," *The Historical Journal* 56 (2013): 909–930, and *Making Archives in Early Modern Europe: Proof, Information and Political Recordkeeping, 1400–1700* (Cambridge: Cambridge University Press, 2019).

For an account of the emergence of historical Pyrrhonism see the classic work by Arnaldo Momigliano, "Ancient History and the Antiquarian," *Journal of the Warburg and Courtauld Institutes* 13 (1950): 285–315; Richard H. Popkin, *The History of Scepticism from Savonarola to Bayle* (rev. ed. Oxford: Oxford University Press, 2003); and the previously mentioned works by Jean-Louis Quantin. A seminal work on the connections between legal theories and the development of the modern historical method remains Donald R. Kelley, *Foundations of Modern Historical Scholarship: Language, Law, and History in the French Renaissance* (New York: Columbia University Press, 1970).

Chapter 7

For an overview of Falconieri's intellectual interests and Roman career see Matteo Sanfilippo's entry devoted to him in the *DBI*. For a synthetic account of Marracci's life and works, see Lisa Saracco's entry in the *DBI*. Marracci's translation of the Qur'an, and, more generally, his approach to the Islamic culture, have been the object of recent scholarly attention. An edition of a portion of Marracci's manuscript translation, together with an analysis of Marracci's linguistic method, have been published by Reinhold F. Glei and Roberto Tottoli in *Ludovico Marracci at Work: The evolution of his Latin translation of the Qur'ān in the light of his newly discovered manuscripts. With an edition and a comparative linguistic analysis of Sura 18* (Wiesbaden: Harrassowitz, 2016). On the cultural, theological, and intellectual significance of Marracci's career as an Arabist see Gian Luca D'Errico, ed., *Il Corano e il Pontefice. Ludovico Marracci fra Cultura Islamica e Curia Papale* (Rome: Carocci, 2015), and for an examination of the role that Marracci and his fellow Christian Arabists played in the relationship between Islam and Christianity see Ziad Elmarsafy, *The Enlightenment Qur'an: the politics of translation and the construction of Islam* (Oxford: Oneworld, 2009), esp. ch.2, and Alexander Bevilacqua, *The Republic of Arabic Letters: Islam and the European Enlightenment* (Cambridge MA: Harvard University Press, 2018). For more context on Marracci's use of probabilist arguments see Tutino, *Uncertainty in Post-Reformation Catholicism. A History of Pobabilism* (Oxford: Oxford University Press, 2018).

On the cultural and intellectual significance of the *plomos* of Granada for the history of post-Tridentine Catholicism see A. Katie Harris, *From Muslim to Christian Granada: Inventing a City's Past in Early Modern Spain* (Baltimore: The Johns Hopkins University Press, 2007) and Mercedes García-Arenal and Ferdinando Rodríguez Mediano, *The Orient in Spain: Converted Muslims, the Forged Lead Books of Granada, and the Rise of Orientalism* (Leiden: Brill, 2013). On the Nestorian monument in the context of the seventeenth-century Jesuit mission to China see David E. Mungello, *Curious Land. Jesuit Accommodation and the Origins of Sinology* (Honolulu: University of Hawaii Press, 1989). For an account of the reception of the Nestorian monument see Michael Keevak, *The Story of a Stele: China's Nestorian Monument and its Reception in the West, 1625–1916* (Hong Kong: Hong Kong University Press, 2008).

On the political, social, and intellectual background of the members of the Papal Curia, and on the impact they had on the wider political and social history of early modern Europe, a good starting point is Mario Rosa, *La Curia Romana nell'Età Moderna. Istituzioni, Cultura, Carriere* (Rome: Viella, 2013). On this topic see also Renata Ago, *Carriere e Clientele nella Roma Barocca* (Bari: Laterza, 1990), Marco Pellegrini, "Corte di Roma e Aristocrazie Italiane in Età Moderna. Per una lettura storico-sociale della Curia romana," *Rivista di storia e letteratura religiosa* 30 (1994): 543–602, and the works by Maria Antonietta Visceglia, especially *Morte e Elezione del Papa. Norme, Riti e Conflitti. L'età moderna* (Roma: Viella, 2013), *Guerra, Diplomacia y Etiqueta en la Corte de los Papas (siglos XVI y XVII)* (Madrid: Ediciones Polifemo, 2010), and *Roma Papale e Spagna. Diplomatici, Nobili e Religiosi tra Due Corti*

(Roma: Bulzoni, 2010). In English, see Gianvittorio Signorotto and Maria Antonietta Visceglia, eds., *Courts and Politics in Papal Rome, 1492–1700* (Cambridge: Cambridge University Press, 2002), and Visceglia, "The Pope's Household and Court in the Early Modern Age," in Jeroen Duindam, Tülay Artan, and Metin Kunt, eds., *Royal Courts in Dynastic States and Empires* (Leiden: Brill, 2011), 239–264.

On the difficulties experienced by the Roman Curia in establishing the authenticity of allegedly miraculous events and charismatic people see the works I mentioned in chapter 2. On the background and implications of the canonization of Francis of Paola, see Ronald C. Finucane, *Contested Canonizations: The Last Medieval Saints, 1482–1523* (Washington, D.C.: The Catholic University of America Press, 2011), ch. 4.

Chapter 8

On the theological, political, and juridical debates concerning crimes of mixed forum, see Paolo Prodi, *Una Storia della Giustizia. Dal Pluralismo dei Fori al Moderno Dualismo tra Coscienza e Giustizia* (Bologna: Il Mulino, 2000); Vincenzo Lavenia, "'Anticamente di Misto Foro'. Inquisizione, Stati e Delitti di Stregoneria nella Prima Età Moderna," in *Inquisizioni: Percorsi di Ricerca*, ed. Giovanna Paolin (Trieste: Edizioni Università di Trieste, 2001), 35–80; Giovanni Romeo, *L'Inquisizione nell'Italia Moderna* (Bari: Laterza, 2002); Marco Bellabarba, *La Giustizia nell'Italia Moderna* (Bari: Laterza, 2008). Among the crimes of mixed forum, witchcraft has definitely seen most scholarly attention, and therefore the bibliography on this topic is abundant and steadily growing. Insofar as the juridical status of witchcraft as a crime of mixed forum is concerned, see, in addition to Lavenia's article, Giovanni Romeo, *Inquisitori, Esorcisti, e Streghe nell'Italia della Controriforma* (Florence: Sansoni, 1990). On the crime of polygamy, which was especially common and controversial in Naples, see Romeo, *Amori Proibiti. I Concubini tra Chiesa e Inquisizione* (Bari: Laterza, 2008); and Pierroberto Scaramella, "Controllo e Repressione Ecclesiastica della Poligamia a Napoli in Età Moderna: dalla Causa Matrimoniale al Crimine di Fede (1514–1799), in *Tragressioni: Seduzione, Concubinato, Adulterio, Bigamia (XIV–XVIII secolo)*, ed. Silvana Seidel Menchi and Diego Quaglioni (Bologna: Il Mulino, 2004), 443–502. For more information on the legal, institutional, jurisdictional, and procedural conflicts between the Roman Inquisition and the political authorities, see the works I mentioned in the bibliographical notes on chapters 1 and 5. For a biography of Lorenzo Brancati di Lauria, see the entry devoted to him in the *DBI*.

As a background on artistic patronage in early modern Italy, Francis Haskell's *Patrons and Painters. Art and Society in Baroque Italy* (New Haven: Yale University Press, 1980), remains a fundamental reference. More recently, Patrizia Cavazzini, *Painting as Business in Seventeenth-Century Rome* (University Park: The Pennsylvania State University Press, 2009), and the collection of essays edited by Richard E. Spear and Philiph Sohm, *Painting for Profit: The Economic Lives of Seventeenth-Century Italian Painters* (New Haven: Yale University Press, 2010), have enabled us to expand significantly our understanding of the social range of those involved in purchasing art and the corresponding importance of painting for the market rather than simply for commission.

For an account of the social, material, and economic conditions in which Neapolitan painters worked, see Christopher R. Marshall, *Baroque Naples and the Industry of Painting. The World in the Workbench* (New Haven: Yale University Press, 2016). For an overview of the viceregal patronage in early modern Naples, see Diana Carrió-Invernizzi, "Royal and Viceregal Art Patronage in Naples (1500–1800), in *A Companion to Early Modern Naples*, ed. Tommaso Astarita, 383–404. For a synthetic account of early modern Neapolitan painters and their biographer Bernardo de' Dominici, see J. Nicholas Napoli, "The Visual Arts," in *A Companion to Early Modern Naples*, ed. Tommaso Astarita, 307–330.

Conclusion

On the topic of fakes and forgeries in general, see Otto Kurz, *Falsi e Falsari* (Venice: Neri Pozza, 1961); Mark Jones ed., *Fake? The Art of Deception* (London: British Museum Press, 1990); Ninina Cuomo di Caprio, *La Galleria dei Falsi: dal Vasaio al Mercato di Antiquariato* (Rome: L'Erma di Bretschneider, 1993); and Umberto Eco, "Tipologia della Falsificazione," in *Fälschungen im Mittelalter*, 5 vols. (Hannover: Monumenta Germaniae Historica, 1988), vol. I, 69–82. Stimulating reflections on the role of history in accounting for change can be found in the last of Richard Southern's four presidential addresses to the Royal Historical Society: "Aspects of the European Tradition of Historical Writing: 1–IV," published in the *Transactions of the Royal Historical Society*, 1971–1973, "Aspects of the European Tradition of Historical Writing 4: The Sense of the Past," *TRHS*, 5th series, 1973, 246–263.

Index